EVERYMAN'S PRAYER BOOK

Democratic Governments and Their
Courts: The Other Great Religions

H. Kenneth MacLennan

EVERYMAN'S PRAYER BOOK
DEMOCRATIC GOVERNMENTS AND THEIR
COURTS: THE OTHER GREAT RELIGIONS

iUniverse books may be ordered through booksellers or by contacting:

iUniverse LLC
1663 Liberty Drive
Bloomington, IN 47403
www.iuniverse.com
1-800-Authors (1-800-288-4677)

ISBN: 978-1-4917-3891-7 (sc)
ISBN: 978-1-4917-3893-1 (hc)
ISBN: 978-1-4917-3892-4 (e)

Library of Congress Control Number: 2014912003

Printed in the United States of America.

iUniverse rev. date: 08/04/2014

CONTENTS

EPIGRAPH

"Not ignorance, but ignorance of ignorance is the death of knowledge." (Alfred North Whitehead)

"All great truths began as blasphemies." (George Bernard Shaw)

Witchcraft is the fraudulent practice of sorcery, or 'crafty science', or the telling of fortunes fraudulently and for consideration (money)*

---

* Criminal Code of Canada, Part IX-Offences and Rights and Property, s. 365. Every one who fraudulently (a) pretends to exercise or to use any kind of witchcraft, sorcery, enchantment or conjuration, (b) undertakes, for a consideration, to tell fortunes, or (c) pretends from his skill in or knowledge of an occult or crafty science to discover where or in what manner anything that is supposed to have been stolen or lost may be found, is guilty of an offence punishable on summary conviction.

PREFACE

Former Archbishop Marcel Gervais, Roman Catholic Diocese of Ottawa, in a piece in the Ottawa Citizen, date unknown, under "ASK THE RELIGION EXPERTS" had this to say about truth. I quote:

> **"The first thing I would say is that every person, no matter what his belief or unbelief, has hold of some truth. No human is completely possessed of error and no religion is totally made up of falsehood. There is always some truth present in every person, and even those of no faith at all possess some truth. Our attitude is to be one of seeking to discover truth anywhere and everywhere."**

The world is replete with conflicts between the world's different religions and conflict between the world's different governments. The world will only be saved from those different conflicts, if believers in religions, and believers in governments better understand the true nature of their religions and governments. Everyman's Prayer Book is my personal search for the truth.

INTRODUCTION

From the beginning of time, religions, governments and their courts have competed as to which was the supreme legitimate authority on proper moral and ethical behavior.

In Everyman's Prayer Book, Part 1, "The Pillars of Christianity in seeking Offerings from Believers", I outline how the Christian religion uses eight foundation and three marketing pillars, and religions generally use many of the same pillars to promote faith in the existence of a supernatural God,and use many of the same elements of the legal definition of witchcraft -fraudulent practice of sorcery or crafty science or fortune telling for consideration (money) in seeking offerings from believers to secure the energy of life, pretending that those in religion are God's agents with insider knowledge on morals and ethics, with special power to prepare man for a hereafter. In outlining the pillars and witchcraft of Christianity, my objective is to save the world. The world will only be saved if clerics in the competition for offerings from believers, separate fact from faith, that their particular religion is the greatest, and the only true religion in the world, otherwise the conflict and atrocities committed in the name of religions will continue.

In Everyman's Prayer Book, Part 11- "The Pillars of Democratic Governments in seeking the Payment of Taxes from Believers", I apply many of the same pillars as used by Christianity in promoting the existence of the Christian God, and son of God to democratic governments, and use many of the same elements of the legal definition of witchcraft -fraudulent practice of sorcery or crafty science or fortune telling for consideration (money) in seeking the payment of taxes from believers. In outlining the pillars and witchcraft of democratic governments my objective is also to save the world. If the world is to be saved from all the atrocities committed in the name of democratic governments, I recommend that politicians separate fact from faith, that individual democratic governments are the greatest governments in the world, otherwise the conflict and atrocities committed in the name of democratic governments in seeking the payment of taxes from believers will continue.

In Everyman's Prayer Book, Part 111- "The Pillars of Democratic Government Courts in Providing Justice to Believers", I apply many of the same pillars and elements of the legal definition of witchcraft as used by Christianity, and democratic governments to believers to the courts in promoting the existence of the secular God, and sons of God for the courts. In outlining the pillars and witchcraft of the courts, my objective is to show that justice in democratic courts, as it is in the courts of all other governments in the world, for the most part is an illusion.

In Everyman's Prayer Book, Part 1V, I make recommendations to democratic governments as to what actions they can take if the world is to be saved from the conflicts between the different religions, and the conflicts between the different governments of the world.

In considering the nature of religions, democratic governments, and their courts you will find important truths and insights into human nature. Those insights and truths will be revealed through satirizing, ridiculing, lampooning, skewering, deflating, dissecting, embarrassing, undressing, unmasking, and exposing the illusion that the crafty science of democracy represents the people, that there is such a thing as real justice in the government's courts, and that those in Christianity, and those in other religions, are agents of God, with insider knowledge on morals and ethics, that have special power to prepare believers for a Hereafter.

Some may think that by applying the legal definition of witchcraft, and applying many of the same pillars of Christianity in Part 1 to Part 11 and Part 111 to show that democratic governments and their courts are also great religions relying upon faith of believers is blasphemous. From satire and humor often eternal truths are revealed about the human condition. By applying the pillars of Christianity, and the elements of witchcraft to the revelations of democratic governments, and their courts, the reader will be able to decide which of the three moral and ethical authorities is the most believable, and has the greatest credibility.

PART 1
THE PILLARS OF CHRISTIANITY IN SEEKING OFFERINGS FROM BELIEVERS

INTRODUCTION

Scientists estimate our world to be about 13 plus billion years old, and our planet Earth about 4.5 billion years old. Single cell life did not begin until about 3.7 billion years ago, shortly after the creation of our planet Earth. Complex multi-cellular life in the form of animals-our precursors, known as tetrapods, with four limbs,that end in a maximum of five fingers and toes, only arose about 400 million years ago; early man six million years ago, and modern man, homo sapiens, only came upon the scene about 200,000 years ago. (Appendix D)

It was only after Homo sapiens, started to move out of Africa, and within the last 10,000 years, after the last major ice age, with the invention of tools, and the domestication of plants and animals, that modern day society began in the fertile crescent (Middle East), and sections of eastern United States, Central and South America, India, China, and Africa, when hunters of fish, fowl, and animals,and gatherers of plants, and fruit, were able to establish small villages or communities, eventually leading to larger chiefdoms and empires. In the early Roman and Greek empires we find the first worship of Gods, such as- our Sun, and the other physical features of our universe.

It was only after the invention of writing about five thousand years ago, that we find the birth of Judaism- worship of one God, in the likeness of man. It was not until about two thousand years ago, that we find the birth and worship of Jesus, and the rise of Christianity, and about fourteen hundred years ago, a revelation from God to Muhammad, and the birth of the Islamic religion. It was only within the last five hundred years, with the invention of the printing press (1450), that the alleged sacred books of Judaism, Christianity and Islam- the Torah, Bible and

Koran, became public knowledge to the masses in competition with each other for offerings from believers, based upon claims of revelations from God.

With the invention of the printing press, we find the spread of knowledge- the beginning of the enlightenment of the masses; the Protestant reformation (1517); Copernicus (1473-1543) plotting the movement of the planets in the heavens, where he believed that the Sun was the center of the universe, and not the Earth,enraging the early Christian Church. The Roman Catholic Church published the Index of Prohibited books to protect the faith and morals of the faithful from reading of immoral books, or works containing theological errors, of which such errors included some scientific works by leading astronomers, such as -Johannes Kepler on the work of Copernicus. In 1600 A.D. Giordano Bruni was burned at the stake by the early Christian Church for suggesting that there were planets and suns in the universe other than our Sun.

In 1609, with the invention of the telescope, and with the improvements made by Galileo in its lens, Galileo was able to plot the actual movement of our sun and planets, and was able to confirm the work of Copernicus that the Sun, indeed, was the center of our local universe, and not the Earth, further enraging the Church, and being placed under house arrest. It was during this same period that we find the colonization of North and South America by the English, French and Spanish, and the founding of the United States of America, Canada, Mexico, and the other countries of Central and South America.

In 1859 Charles Darwin published his work on the origin of species, providing a scientific explanation for the evolution of man by natural selection, and the Church's claim that the first man and woman was Adam and Eve, became to be questioned. It was during this same period in our history, that Sir Isaac Newton provided his theory of gravity. Later in the early 1900's Albert Einstein confirmed Newton's theory of gravity, but provided a different explanation of gravity- that gravity resulted from the motion of the stars and planets in the heavens warping the space of those same stars and planets.

It was not until 1923, when Edwin Hubble discovered that there were other constellations, galaxies, and suns outside of our local universe, and the world was much greater than originally thought, as Giordano Bruni had earlier speculated, and that the Church sinned in 1600 in burning Giordano Bruni at the stake for suggesting that there were other planets and suns in the universe. It was not until Hubble's later discovery that the universe was expanding, that it was determined that neither the Sun, nor Earth were at the center of the universe, as with an expanding universe there could be no center of the universe.

It was not until 1964 that scientists were able to find evidence that the universe had a beginning, known as the Big Bang, in the discovery of a faint radiation hiss throughout the whole universe, where it was theorized that the universe began as a tiny bubble at high temperature, experienced a burst of inflation, expanded, and as the universe expanded, it began to cool, currently to a temperature 2.73 degrees above absolute zero. It was only recently with improvements in the telescope that scientists have been able to see the light, that was emitted shortly after the Big Bang. Scientists now believe that they have found the Higg's boson, the "God particle" that provides mass to the electron and proton, and all the other particles in the universe, including life.

Does the evidence for the Big Bang mean that there is no basis for the speculation and make believe of Christianity, or any of the other religions on the existence of God? No!! Neither science, nor religion are able to explain how our world was created from nothing, how life was created based upon the carbon atom, and thought and emotion result from chemical or atomic processes. Until the causes of those three unknowns are found, religion will continue to be able to engage in its speculation and make believe on the existence of God, and science will be able to continue to search for the evidence that will explain the cause of the initial creation event, the cause for the origin of life based upon the carbon atom, and the atomic, or chemical processes giving rise to thought and emotion.

THE CHRISTIAN BUSINESS PLAN

There is a reasonable basis for the business of religion,as there are three unknowns- the cause of the creation of the universe, the cause for the origin of life from the carbon atom, and how thinking and emotion can result from the chemical interaction of atoms or elements within our bodies. My concern, however, is has Christianity's speculation and make believe, in the competition for offerings from believers, crossed the line between faith and fact, and by crossing that fine line encouraged religious fanaticism, resulting in many of the atrocities committed by religion in modern day society.

To answer that question, I look specifically at the business of Christianity. As Roman Catholicism is the father of Christianity, and Christianity is the world's largest religion, and the Roman Catholic religion is the only religion that has an extensive written record in seeking offerings from believers, I use the Roman Catholic business plan as found in Matthew Bunson, General Editor, 2010 Catholic Almanac, as my main source of information, including information from the Christian Bible in outlining the pillars of Christianity in seeking offerings from believers.

You will find from Robert W. Funk, in book titled "The Acts of Jesus, The Search for the Authentic Deeds of Jesus" a different story from that in the Bible, and the Roman Catholic Almanac. The seventy-nine internationally recognized biblical scholars, representative of the different Christian traditions, reporting as religious historians, and not as theologians, whose task it is to promote their business, and who must depend upon offerings in order to secure the food energy, necessities, and comforts of life, relocate the gospels to myths and stories. You will find that the Roman Catholic Church over time has also accepted much of the science on the creation of the universe and evolution of man, contrary to the stories as reported in the Bible.

The purpose of all businesses in society is to seek money from believers in order to secure the food energy necessary for life produced by our Sun. The business of religion is no different from other businesses, although believers may believe it is more special, as it deals with ethics and morals, and our salvation. Our forebears, as hunters and gatherers, secured their food energy by hunting for animals and fowl, and by fishing, and gathering of fruits and plants, and engaged in trading, or exchanging or sharing their food energy with others. With the invention of tools and domestication of animals, a more settled and complex society arose, where the work necessary to secure the food energy and shelter for life became subdivided among different segments of society, each performing a different task in order to secure this food energy and shelter.

In our early history it was the feudal system that served this purpose, where a chief or lord, in return for protection of his subjects, received that food energy from the toil of his subjects. Later with the development of property rights, individuals did not have to depend upon a chief, but could become a landholder, and provide their own shelter, and produce their own food energy, and sell any surplus food energy to those who had established other businesses in society, or exchange their products and services for the products and services of the other businesses. To facilitate the process of exchange or transfer of goods and services, coinage developed, including the use of paper money.

In modern times this transfer or exchange of goods and services becomes the lifeblood for the creation of different businesses in society. A grocery store owner uses the money received from your purchases to pay his employees for their service, cover the cost of products that you purchase, and to cover the costs of his operation as a business, including his life's shelter and food energy needs. In a similar fashion, a bank sells the service of depositing your money. You receive the product, or benefit from your deposit in the form of interest. The bank uses your deposited money to lend to other customers and receives the product, or the benefit of interest in return from other customers. The bank uses the proceeds, or interest from selling its product (your money) to provide its employees the reward of money for their service. Shareholders of the bank, in part, use the profits (interest and dividends) earned by the bank to secure the food energy and shelter necessary for life.

The business of religion has the same need for money or offerings from believers to secure the energy and shelter needs of clerics, as does the other businesses in society. In order for those in the business of religion to secure the food energy, clothing, shelter, and other essentials necessary for life, they seek offerings from their believers for providing the service of preparation for the Hereafter. Religion may have been our first great capitalist enterprise, competing with those in other religion businesses, and other non religion businesses for our offerings. In the competition among the different religion businesses for our offerings, each religion differentiates itself from other religious businesses, primarily in the content of their sacred books, and the type of sorcery, or magic, ritual and ceremony used to market their business.

At the core of religion's business plan is convincing believers in the existence of God, and that those in religion are agents of God. As no one has seen, or heard from God, religion needs some concrete evidence for God's existence. A revelation from God becomes that evidence, as the one supernatural God, external to the universe, all powerful, all perfect, and all knowing. Obeying God's Commands, becomes necessary, if one is to be saved, and enter the supernatural world- known in western society as Heaven.

For Judaism, the proof of God's existence is found in the revelation of the Torah from the prophet Moses on Mount Sinai, about 1600 B.C. where Jews would become God's chosen people. For Christianity, the revelation occurs in the New Testament, about two thousand years ago, with Christianity piggy backing its New Testament, on the Old Testament from the Jewish Torah, claiming Jesus to be the son of God. For Islam, the revelation of the Koran comes to the prophet Mohammed, as a messenger of God, about six hundred years after the beginning of Christianity - the true religion of Adam, Abraham, Moses and Jesus. For Bahai, the revelation of the Kitab-i-Aqdas comes to the prophet Baha'u'llah, about two hundred years from the present in a dream in the dungeon of a black pit in Tehran, located in present day Iran. For Bahai, Moses is succeeded by Jesus Christ, who is succeeded by Muhammad, and Muhammad is succeeded by Baha'u'llah, making Bahai the true religion of God- the successor of all the religions.

It was not until the invention of the printing press, five hundred or so years ago, after earlier resistance of clerics, that the different revelations of the Bible, Torah, Koran, and Kitab-i-Aqdas became available to the masses. Over time those revelations, alleged from God, changed as a result of different interpretations of their original revelations, for example -Judaism becomes reform, conservative, and orthodox- Islam, as Sunni and Shia, and Christianity, as Eastern Orthodox, Roman Catholicism, and Protestantism, which further splinters into its many different sects reflecting different interpretations of the original revelation, or written word.

Central to instilling belief in each religion's business plan is the memorization of its particular catechism and creed. As the young are the future makers of offerings, each religion focuses on instilling belief in the young, that it is the true religion of God, through Sunday school, Bible schools, Bible camps, and journeys to the father. This includes establishing their own religious schools, if unable to convince the State to fund their religion. The goal of all religions is to recruit and convert those of other religions to support their business, in order to increase their offerings, and thereby enhance the quality of life of their workers. To do so they pretend to be agents of God, with special powers in providing the service of preparation for a hereafter in a make believe supernatural world.

Part 1 -The Pillars of Christianity in seeking offerings from believers will hopefully end some of that ignorance by providing believers with a bare bones look at religion as a business, like the government,and all the other businesses in society-selling a service, or a product to secure the money necessary to obtain the food energy, shelter, and all the other amenities of life, although believers may believe the business of religion is more special, as it deals with ethics and morals, and our salvation. To secure this food energy, and all the other necessities of life, whereas most businesses charge for their services, or products, the businesses of religion seek voluntary offerings, or resort to begging.

Eleven pillars constitute the bare bones of the Christian business plan. Eight are foundation pillars based upon faith, and three are marketing pillars used in promotion of the eight foundation pillars. You will find evidence that Christianity uses many of the same elements as found in the legal definition of witchcraft, for example- crafty science, when as non-scientists the early writers of the Bible state that God created the universe, and that the first man and woman were Adam and Eve. You will find evidence that Christian clerics use sorcery (magic, ritual and ceremony) to create the impression that they are agents of God.

You will find evidence of Christian clerics telling fortunes fraudulently, when they seek offerings (consideration) from believers promoting that if you obey God's commands, you will be saved in a Hereafter, but provide no evidence of a Hereafter. (Criminal Code of Canada, Part IX-Offences and Rights and Property, s. 365. Every one who fraudulently (a) pretends to exercise or to use any kind of witchcraft, sorcery, enchantment or conjuration, (b) undertakes, for a consideration, to tell fortunes, or (c) pretends from his skill in or knowledge of an occult or crafty science to discover where or in what manner anything that is supposed to have been stolen or lost may be found, is guilty of an offence punishable on summary conviction.)

CHRISTIANITY'S EIGHT FOUNDATION PILLARS

1. Pillar of Faith in Existence of God

The 2010 Roman Catholic Almanac acknowledges that the existence of God is an article of faith. I quote:

> **God: "The existence of God is an article of faith, clearly communicated in divine Revelation. The infinitely perfect Supreme Being uncaused and absolutely self-sufficient, eternal, the Creator and end of all things. The one God subsists in three equal persons, the Father and the Son, and the Holy Spirit.** (Bunson, God, P 143)

The Almanac further states that faith is the norm or standard of religious belief. I quote:

> **Rule of Faith: The norm or standard of religious belief. The Catholic doctrine is that belief must be professed in the divinely revealed truths in the Bible and tradition, as interpreted and proposed by the infallible teaching authority of the Church.** (Bunson, P. 141)

2. Pillar of Faith That Jesus Is the Son of God.

I quote from the Bible, Luke, verses 26 to 35 on the virgin birth, and divinity of Jesus as the son of God.

26- [In the sixth month the angel Gabriel was sent from God to a city of Galilee named Nazareth 27 to a virgin betrothed to a man whose name was Joseph, of the house of David; and the virgin's name was Mary. 28 And he came to her and said, "Hail, O favoured one, the Lord is with you!" 29 But she was greatly troubled at the saying, and considered in her mind what sort of greeting this might be. 30 And the angel said to her, "Do not be afraid, Mary, for you have found favour with God. 31 And behold, you will conceive in your womb and bear a son, and you shall call his name Jesus. 32 He will be great, and will be called the Son of the Most High; 34 And Mary said to the angel, "How shall this be, since I have no husband?" 35 And the angel said to her, "The Holy Spirit will come upon you, and the power of the Most High will overshadow you; therefore the child to be born will be called holy,the Son of God."]

3. Pillar of Faith That God Created the World

I quote in part from the book of Genesis 1, verse 1:

"In the beginning God created the heavens and the earth. The earth was without form and void, and darkness was upon the face of the deep; and the spirit of God was moving over the face of the waters.

4. Pillar of Faith That God Created the First Man and Woman- Adam and Eve

On God creating the first man and women- Adam and Eve, I quote Genesis 1: verses 26 and 27:

"Then God said, "Let us make man to our image, after our likeness; and let them have dominion over the fish of the sea, and over the birds of the air, and over the cattle, and over all the earth, and over every creeping thing that creeps upon the earth "So God created man in his own image, in the image of God he created him; male and female he created them."

5. Pillar of Faith That the Bible Contains the Word of God

The common practice in Christian churches is to make the claim that the Bible is the word of God.

6. Pillar of Faith That the Bible's Morals and Ethics Are the Laws of God.

The Bible's morals and ethics include the Ten Commandments, the Beatitudes, and Christian Virtues (Appendix A). I quote the Ten Commandments:

"1. You shall love no other gods before me.

2. You shall not make for yourself an idol, or any likeness of what is in heaven above or on the earth beneath or in the water under the earth.

3. You shall not take the name of the Lord your God in vain, for the Lord will not leave him unpunished who takes His name in vain.

4. Remember the Sabbath day to make it holy.

5. Honour your father and your mother, that your days may be prolonged in the land which the Lord your God gives you.

6. You shall not murder.

7. You shall not commit adultery.

8. You shall not steal.

9. You shall not bear false witness against your neighbour.

10. You shall not covet your neighbour's house; you shall not covet your neighbour's wife or his male servant or his female servant or his ox or his donkey or anything that belongs to your neighbour."

Source: Christian Bible, Exodus, chapter 20, verses 3, 4, 7, 8 and 12-17 and Deuteronomy, chapter 5, verses 7,8,11,12 and 16-21.

Jesus reduced the law of the Ten Commandments to two Commandments, as found in Matthew 22:37-40 as follows. I quote:

"Love the Lord thy God with all thy heart, and all thy soul, with all thy mind. This is the first and greatest Commandment. And the second is like unto it: Love thy neighbour as thyself."

In the Beatitudes, Christianity provides the following guidance on virtues in living a good life. I quote Matthew 5:3-12:

"Blessed are the poor in spirit, for theirs is the kingdom of heaven.

"Blessed are those who mourn, for they shall be comforted.

"Blessed are the meek, for they shall inherit the earth.

"Blessed are those who hunger and thirst for righteousness, for they shall be satisfied.

"Blessed are the merciful, for they shall obtain mercy.

"Blessed are the pure in heart, for they shall see God.

"Blessed are the peacemakers, for they shall be called sons of God.

"Blessed are those who are persecuted for righteousness' sake, for theirs is the kingdom of heaven.

"Blessed are you when men revile you, and persecute you, and utter all kinds of evil against you, falsely on my account.

"Rejoice and be glad, for your reward is great in heaven, for so men persecuted the prophets who were before you.

7. Pillar of Faith in Fortune Telling That If You Obey God's Laws You Will Be Saved in a Hereafter

I quote from the 2010 Roman Catholic Almanac on the crafty science for the existence of a Hereafter:

> **Salvation: The liberation of persons from sin, and it effects, reconciliation with God in and through Christ, the attainment of union with God forever in the glory of heaven, as the supreme purpose of life, and as the God-given reward for the fulfillment of his will on earth.** (Bunson, P. 155, in part)

The Almanac further states that to gain salvation, it is necessary to be a member of the Roman Catholic Church and participate in the Church for salvation. I quote from the Church's Dogmatic Constitution:

> **"the necessity of membership and participation in the Church for salvation."** (Bunson, P. 89)

And what is heaven? I quote:

> **Heaven: The state of those who, having achieved salvation, are in glory with god and enjoy the beatific vision. The phrase kingdom of heaven refers to the order or kingdom of God, grace, salvation.** (Bunson, P. 143)

And what is this beatific vision. According to the Roman Catholic business plan, it is a supernatural mystery. I quote (Bunson again, P. 132):

Beatific Vision: The intuitive, immediate and direct vision and experience of God enjoyed in the light of glory by all the blessed in heaven. The vision is a supernatural mystery.

And what are the penalties if you are not good and disobey God, the Almanac states that there are two kinds of punishment for sin.

"Eternal punishment is the punishment of hell, to which one becomes subject by the commission of mortal sin. Such punishment is remitted when mortal sin is forgiven.

Temporal punishment is a consequence of venial sin and or forgiven sin; it is not everlasting and may be remitted in this life by means of penance. Temporal punishment unremitted during this life is remitted by suffering in purgatory."(Bunson, Punishment Due to Sin, p. 165)

And if you sin, you will go to hell. I quote:

Hell: The state of persons who die in mortal sin, in a condition of self-alienation from God which will last forever. (Bunson, P. 143)

8. Pillar of Faith That in Prayer You Connect with God

In the marketing of Christianity, the Lord's Prayer becomes the main medium for believers in connecting with God. It is the Lord's Prayer that instills belief in the existence, and divinity of God, the existence of a Hereafter, and as an appeal to God to save man from evil. I quote:

Our Father in heaven,
Thy name be hallowed;
Thy kingdom come,
Thy will be done,
On earth as in heaven.
Give us today our daily bread.
Forgive us the wrong we have done,
As we have forgiven those who have wronged us.

And do not bring us to the test,
But save us from the evil one.
For thine is the kingdom
And the power and the glory, for ever.
Amen

The recitation of the Apostle's creed serves the same purpose as the recitation of the Lord's Prayer in indoctrinating believers in the truth of Christianity's business plan, as a means in seeking offerings from believers. The Apostle's creed summarizes the foundation upon which the Christian business plan is based and is recited at special times to remind believers that God created heaven and earth, and that his only son Jesus Christ sitteth on the right hand of God, the Father Almighty, conceived by the holy spirit, born of the Virgin Mary, who will come to judge the quick and dead. If you believe in the Holy Spirit, and the forgiveness of sins, you will achieve life everlasting. (Bunson, Apostle's Creed, p. 124) I quote:

> "I believe in God the Father Almighty
> Maker of heaven and earth;
> And in Jesus Christ his only Son our Lord
> Who was conceived by the Holy Spirit,
> Born of the Virgin Mary,
> Suffered under Pontius Pilate,
> Was crucified, dead and buried;
> He descended into hell;
> The third day he arose again from the dead;
> He ascended into heaven
> And sitteth on the right hand of God the Father Almighty;
> He shall come to judge the quick and dead.
> I believe in the Holy Spirit, the holy Catholic church,
> The communion of saints,
> The forgiveness of sins,
> The resurrection of the body,
> And the life everlasting,
> Amen."

CHRISTIANITY'S THREE MARKETING PILLARS

If proof for the existence of the Christian God is faith in the Bible, written by men, inspired by the Holy Spirit (dove and tongues of fire), and all the business plans of the other religions rests solely upon faith in their sacred books, how does each religion convince believers that they are agents of God? They do so by the aid of three marketing pillars - the worship of idols, pilgrimages to one's holy places, and the use of crafty science (sorcery or magic, and ritual and ceremony).

1. The Pillar of Worship of Idols to Convince Believers That Those in Religion Are Agents of God

The worship of idols takes the form of the worship of Moses, Muhammad, Baha'u'llah, Jesus Christ, and all the other saints and idols of religion. The Roman Catholic Church has an elaborate system for determining the future saints of their religion based upon belief in performance of miracles, good works and strong morals.

2. The Pillar of Pilgrimages to One's Holy Places to Convince Believers That Those in Religion Are Agents of God

Periodic pilgrimages are made to Jerusalem, Bethlehem, Nazareth, the Vatican, Canterbury, Constantinople, Mt. Athos, Mecca and Medina and the various other such places deemed holy by a religion to re-enforce belief in God, and the truth of his or her revelation.

3. The Pillar of Sorcery or Crafty Science to Convince Believers That Those in Religion Are Agents of God

This witchcraft is described as cult by John L. McKenzie, SJ, in his book, "The Roman Catholic Church", p.124-124 and 126. I quote:

> "**Roman Catholicism is a society which practices ritual cult, and it attaches great importance to the cult. Its first element is that cult in many religions is believed to have been instituted by the deity directly or through an accredited mediator. Thus, in Judaism, the cultic institutions were attributed to Moses, and in Roman Catholicism, the basic rites were attributed to the institution of Jesus Christ.**
>
> **The second element in the rational basis is the symbolic value of the rite. The basic symbol is the word, and cultic language employs words, but this is not the symbolism which is properly ritual. Cult is not merely the recitation of words but also the performance of actions, and the symbol of the action is not as self-evident as the symbol of the word. Ritual cult is social, performed in a group for a group. The sacraments are the major ritual actions of the Catholic Church, and the Roman idea of their symbolism has no real parallel in other religions.**"

THE ROMAN CATHOLIC CHURCH REVISES ITS BUSINESS PLAN

With the advances in science providing new knowledge on the evolution of the universe, the Roman Catholic Church acknowledges that the writers of the Bible did not write as scientists, but as communicator's of religious truth. I quote from the 2010 Roman Catholic Almanac :

> "So far as the Genesis account of creation is concerned, the Catholic view is that the writer (s) did not write as a scientist, but as the communicator of religious truth in the manner adapted to the understanding of the people of his time." "It was beyond the competency and purpose of the writer (s) to describe creation and related events in a scientific manner." (Bunson, Evolution, P 140)

The 2010 Roman Catholic Almanac accepts the scientific evidence on the evolution of species. I quote, in part:

> "Various ideas about evolution were advanced for some centuries before scientific evidence in support of the main-line theory of organic evolution, which has several formulations, was discovered and verified in the second half of the 19th century and afterwards. This evidence- from the findings of comparative anatomy and other sciences- confirmed evolution of species -----. "(Bunson, Evolution, P 140)

The Roman Catholic Church acknowledges that the Bible contains the words of men, under the inspiration of the Holy Spirit. I quote:

> **"The canon of the Bible is the Church's official list of sacred writings. These works, written by men under the inspiration of the Holy Spirit, contain divine revelation and, in conjunction with tradition and teaching authority of the Church, constitute the rule of the Catholic faith** (Bunson, P. 96)

What is this Christian Holy Spirit that inspired the writers? I quote, in part:

> **Holy Spirit: God the Holy Spirit, third Person of the Holy Trinity, who proceeds from the Father and the Son, and with him, he is equal and every respect; inspirer of the prophets and writers of Sacred Scripture; appeared in the form of a dove at the baptism of Christ and as tongues of fire at his descent upon the Apostles; soul of the Church and guarantor, by his abiding presence and action, of truth in doctrine----.** (Bunson, P. 144)

To believe that the Bible is the words of God written by men inspired by a holy spirit, one must believe that a dove and tongues of fire communicated God's words to men.

THE BIBLE AS GOD'S LAWS

All religions compete with government as to proper moral and ethical behavior. The center of religion's business plan is the claim of insider knowledge on morals and ethics. Why do religions claim to have insider knowledge on morals and ethics? To enhance their power in seeking offerings from believers, each religion creates the impression that its clerics are agents of God, and for some religions, that the clerics to have special powers in forgiving sin- that regular church, mosque, or temple attendance, and offerings are necessary to gain entry into Heaven, none of which is based upon any evidence, that religion's speculation is true.

In religion's pretense to have power, it mimics the government and legal profession in its dress to create awe and respect. Some will argue that religion outdoes the legal profession, and all the kings and queens of the world in its majesty. Religion creates the pretense, that it is their ethics and morals, that are the true laws of God, and that they supersede the laws of the State. The intent of those laws is to create the impression that clerics in religion have real power. If you believe that religion has real power, you will be more likely to obey their laws, and make offerings to support their businesses.

Three of the most popular moral and ethical frameworks in determining right and wrong are duty based, consequentialist, and virtue based theories. For the negatives and positives of those three theories the reader is referred to Warburton, pages 40-60. Christian morals and ethics are both duty based and virtue based. When duty based they include actions that ought to be taken, or not taken, regardless of the consequences.

The Ten Commandments are duty based commands. The first four are basically hero worship and have little moral implications, for example- you shall not take the name of the Lord your God in vain; remember to make the Sabbath day holy; you shall love no other Gods; you shall not make yourself an idol, or any likeness of what is in heaven above, earth beneath, or in water under the earth. The last six have moral and ethical implications: you shall not commit murder, commit adultery, or steal; you must honour your father and mother; you shall not bear false witness against your neighbour; you shall not covet your neighbour's house; you shall not covet your neighbour's wife, or his male servant or his female servant, or his ox, or his donkey or anything that belongs to your neighbour.

The first and greatest Christian commandment is found in Matthew 22:37-40

"Love the Lord thy God with all thy heart, and all thy soul, with all thy mind"

Although duty based it is primarily hero worship of God, and Jesus as the son of God - the moral implication being, that if you do not worship God, and Jesus, you will not be saved. The second greatest commandment is both duty based, and virtue based. How shall I live?

"Love thy neighbour as thyself."

The Beatitudes and the other virtues in the Christian Bible (Appendix A) do not provide any guidance on practising the virtues in one's daily living. However, they do identify virtues for the most part, worthy of following. What the Beatitudes do is primarily support religion's fortune telling of the existence of God and heaven, for example - blessed are those poor in spirit for theirs is the kingdom of heaven ; blessed are those who mourn for they shall be comforted; blessed are the meek for they shall inherit the earth; blessed are those who hunger for righteousness sake for theirs is the kingdom of heaven; blessed are those who are merciful for they shall obtain mercy; blessed are those who are peacemakers for they shall be the sons of God; blessed are those pure in heart, for they shall see God; blessed are you, when men revile you, and persecute you- rejoice for your reward is great in heaven.

Consequentialist based ethical theories,on the other hand, are not duty based, or virtue based, but focus on judgement as to whether an action is right or wrong, not on the intentions of the person performing the action, but on the consequences of his action. In Christianity, whereas it is a duty to not murder or steal, in a consequentialist based theory, it would be what happened, as a result of the murder or stealing, that would determine whether the murder or stealing was right or wrong. For example -murder would be acceptable in a war, if the murder served the greater good of society, and stealing would be acceptable if it served the greater good. Being dishonest or lying would be acceptable if it serves the common good of the greater number of persons in society.

The Ten Commandments, Beatitudes and virtues in the Bible provide no insider knowledge on morals and ethics. The reality, from the record of history often shows that Christianity's rules or laws, as absolute commands in the social domain change to reflect the current wisdom of society. For example- slavery, discrimination of blacks, women as non persons, and discrimination of homosexuals is considered unacceptable today in many parts of modern society, although the Roman Catholic Church still considers homosexuality as a sin. In democratic countries, where there are those of many religions, including those of no religion, the State quite properly becomes the ultimate determiner of right and wrong, reflecting the pre-eminence of the State in morals and ethics over any particular morals and ethics of a particular religion.

The Roman Catholic Church has an elaborate system of canon laws and courts, but the laws and courts primarily deal with infractions by believers of the business plan of the Church, and not the Ten Commandments, Beatitudes, or Christian virtues. The only Roman Catholic law penalties are denial of the sacraments, excommunication, refusal to marry a divorced person, or perform some other service, or stripping a religious institution from its religious designation, if it performs an act contrary to the Church's doctrine. In countries predominantly Christian, it is the morals and ethics of the State, often reflecting Christian morals and ethics, that is the supreme law of the country. On the contrary, in many Islamic countries, where the Islamic religion is the State religion, it is the religious law that is the supreme law of the country in its courts.

CHRISTIANITY'S CRAFTY SCIENCE

When religion fortune tells of a heaven, and seeks offerings for its service of preparation for a hereafter, and provides no evidence of the hereafter in seeking offerings from believers, is it not telling fortunes fraudulently? The late Pope John 1I acknowledged that heaven and hell were states of mind, and not physical places. Is it not crafty science when Christianity promotes that in prayer you connect with God,without evidence that God responds to your prayer, and that the virgin birth of Jesus, as the son of God, resulted from impregnation by a Holy Spirit?

I have no problem with sorcery and magic (ritual and ceremony) in baptism, the sacraments of marriage, and death, and in communion - a celebration of the power of its leader, or hero, through the use of beads, incense, holy water, sermons, homilies, scripture readings, hymns, music, art, symbols, forms of dress, chanting, and so on, as it can be uplifting for believers in religion.

Sorcery can also be found, in the competition for offerings among the different religions, when religions differentiate themselves from the other religious businesses, by providing distinct symbols, such as the cross, star of David, crescent moon, and in their many practices to separate themselves from the other religious businesses, hoping that their particular symbols and practices will gain the favor of believers. Christians worship on Sunday, Jews on Saturday, and Muslims on Friday. Muslims prostrate themselves in prayer. Some Christians kneel. Other Christians sit and bow their heads. Jews stand.

It is the use of sorcery or magic that creates the impression to believers that each religion is special, the true religion of God, however, that incites all the atrocities committed in the name of their religion, as it does for government through the use of its sorcery in the use of flags, symbols, national anthems, and oaths of allegiance, promoting the special ness of each country, or nation state, that incites wars against other countries or nation states. When the messages of religion are presented, as fact, and not as speculation, it incites believers to fanaticism. The challenge for all religions is how do they use their sorcery and magic, without creating the impression that they are agents of God with special powers, and insider knowledge on morals and ethics.

WHO IS RECEIVING THE GREATEST BENEFIT?

Why do you make an offering? You must believe that those in religion are agents of God, with insider knowledge on morals and ethics, and if you obey God's laws, you will be saved in a Hereafter. Making an offering, you become a shareholder in the business of your religion. Review the financial statements of your church, temple or mosque. Who is receiving the greatest benefit from your offerings? You, the poor, sick, disadvantaged, your priest, minister, rabbi or imam?

Your priest, minister, rabbi or imam receive a church, temple or mosque, to conduct their business, including offerings to cover operation and maintenance expenses, and the money necessary to purchase the food energy necessary for life, and life's shelter and other amenities.

You receive a weekly religious service worshipping God, advice on moral and ethical behaviour, and if you request, you receive celebrations of birth, marriage, and death, piggy backing on the States official registration of births, marriages and deaths.

As a charity providing a tax receipt for your offerings, has a substantial portion of your offerings provided a material benefit to the poor, sick, and disadvantaged, or has the major portion just gone to support the capital, operating and maintenance costs of the business, and for the personal support of your priest, minister, rabbi or imam? If the government did not provide a reduction in income tax for your offerings, would you continue to provide offerings to support your church, temple or mosque?

CHRISTIAN SCHOLARS TELL
A DIFFERENT STORY

Christian religious scholars in the book titled **"The Acts of Jesus", The Search for the Authentic Deeds of Jesus**", Robert W. Funk, editor in chief, provides a much different story of Christianity, than does the business of Christianity. "The Acts of Jesus" is a report of more than seventy-nine internationally recognized biblical scholars, representative of the different Christian traditions, who as religious historians do not need to depend upon offerings for life's food and energy, as does your local priest or minister, whose task it is to promote their business, and must depend upon offerings from believers in order to secure the food energy, necessities, and comforts of life.

The methodology used by the Christian biblical scholars in arriving at their conclusions is known as the principle of multiple attestations. An act or event is found to be more likely to be true, if confirmed or verified by similar reports of others, with the degree of probability of truth, based upon the number of such independent confirmations. If confirmations are found outside the Christian belief system, from other historical sources, the degree of probability would be increased. (Funk, Introduction, p. 1-40)

> **"They examined 387 reports of 176 events and 69 versions of 47 narrative summaries, transitions, asides, generalized settings, and lists".** (Funk, preface, P xi)

"The earliest substantial physical evidence for the gospels comes from the end of the second century C.E. about 170 years after Jesus' demise". *(Funk, p. 2)*

"In the manufacture and maintenance of folklore, memory does not function like a videotape. It is not possible to rewind and replay one's memories. On the contrary, memories are constantly edited, deleted, augmented, and combined with other memories as persons call them to mind. And when one adds the element of fear, or paranoia, or conviction, or nostalgia, those memories can become more vivid and powerful than everyday life". *(Funk, p. 6)*

Of the twenty some gospels surviving, either in whole, or in part, in the first three centuries of the common era (C.E.), only four were included in the New Testament. Obviously it was only those four that best served Christianity's business plan. (Funk P. 38-40)

On the claim that Jesus was born of the Virgin Mary, and is the son of God, the Scholars concluded that the virgin birth was not a biological statement, but a theological statement. I quote from the Acts of Jesus:

"With regard to the manner of Jesus' conception, the Fellows were unequivocal. With a virtually unanimous vote, the Fellows declared that the statement 'Jesus was conceived of the holy spirit' is a theological and not a biological statement". (Funk, p. 504)

"In view of the nature of the appearances and the late emergence of stories representing the resurrection as physical and palatable, the Seminar concluded:"

"The body of Jesus decayed as do other corpses." (Funk, p. 462)

According to the Jesus Seminar:

"Jesus practised healing without the use of ancient medicine or magic relieving afflictions we now consider psychosomatic. He did not walk on water, feed the multitude with loaves and fishes, change water into wine, or raise Lazurus from the dead. He was executed as a public nuisance, not for claiming to be the son of God." (Funk, Jacket)

On the need for humans to live not only by the bread of facts alone, and the need for stories or myths to make sense of life, I quote, in part, from the Acts of Jesus titled "Redeeming the myths" (Funk, P 534)

"The fellows of the Jesus Seminar are profoundly cognizant that human beings do not live by the bread of facts alone. Exposing them (gospels) **to historical assessment relocates them in the realm of story and myth, so that they can recover their proper function."**

This report of the seventy-five learned religious scholars, representative of the different Christian traditions, who one might expect would want to believe Christianity's claim, is particularly troubling for the business of Christianity, which relies on belief in the deity of Jesus, as the son of God, as the center of its business plan, in seeking offerings to support its business.

In the Christian business plan, the existence of God is unknown, supported only by revelation- the Bible, as words by men inspired through a Holy Spirit (Dove and tongues of fire). The existence of Jesus, as the son of God, through a virgin birth, is also only supported through the same Holy Spirit. Obviously those in the business of Christianity, who depend upon collections from believers, do not agree with the report of Christian religious scholars, who do not depend upon the collection plate for sustenance. Such report of Christian religious scholars questions the foundation, and places in jeopardy the whole marketplace of Christianity. The report of Christian religious scholars is obviously not good news for the promoters of the Christian religion.

RELIGION AND THE ADVERTISING LAW

Section 52 (1) (a) of the *Competition Act*, Government of Canada, is the general prohibition against misleading deceptive advertising, where it is not necessary for the Crown to prove that any person was in fact misled, only that the representation was capable of misleading.

The Federal Trade Act, Government of the United States, provides similar admonitions to businesses, as the Canadian law, in advertising their products and services as found in a *FTC Policy Statement on Deception*, provided in a letter by James C. Millar 111, Chairman, dated October 13,1983, to Honourable John D. Dingell, Chairman, Committee on Energy & Commerce, United States House of Representatives. Commission policy makes the following admonitions. I quote:

> **"At common law, a consumer can generally rely on an expert opinion. For this reason representations on an expert opinion will generally be regarded as representations of fact"**

Many believers regard priests, ministers, rabbis and imams, as experts, and therefore their pronouncements, as fact. Believers need to be reminded, that the purveyors of religion are not experts, but simply speculators on the existence of God, including morals and ethics.

> **"The term puffing refers generally to an expression of opinion not made as a representation of fact."**

Religion must separate faith (puffing) from fact in promotion of its religion, otherwise it misleads believers.

> **"no claim of association with, authorization by, or relationship to a third party, should be made, unless true. If no agreement exists between the advertiser and the third party, this is a good indication that such a claim should not be made."**

In confession, in the Roman Catholic Church, a priest pretends to be an agent of God with power to forgive sin. I quote from the Roman Catholic Almanac:

> **Confession: Sacramental confession is the act by which a person tells or confesses his sins to a priest who is authorized to give absolution in the sacrament of penance.** (Bunson, P. 136)

And what is Absolution, sacramental?

> **Absolution, Sacramental: The act by which bishops and priests acting as agents of Christ and ministers of the church, grant forgiveness of sins in the sacrament of penance.** (Bunson, P. 128)

Where is the evidence of a formal agreement between the Roman Catholic religion, as the advertiser, and God, as the third party, that priests of the Roman Catholic religion are agents of God, who in confession have the power to forgive sin?

RELIGION AS SPECULATION AND MAKE BELIEVE

Religion as a Security Blanket

What is there about the psychology of the human mind that causes many humans to believe in a supernatural God without evidence? The answer to that question for many humans is found in the cultural indoctrination passed down from family to family in society thru the ages, in response to the business practices of religion. This does not explain, however, the basic human quality that would give rise to belief in a God. Would such belief be a sign of weakness, or insecurity in the human spirit, which religion satisfies? Would it be because many humans are unable to accept death, and religion, is a security blanket for the insecure? Or do those who are religious see something that others are unable to understand or fathom? What is their about the psychology of the mind that would cause some to believe without evidence, and others to disbelieve?

The will to believe is so strong for those who do believe, that you could make up anything, and it would be believed. The sad part of it all is that those in religion do not need to engage in false, or misleading advertising to secure the food energy for life. If honesty prevailed, religion would still continue to thrive. The only thing that would suffer is the decline of religious fanaticism and extremism. It is when religious clerics refer to God, as if they are his agent, with insider knowledge of God's wishes or commands, and that their religion is the only one true religion, that fanaticism and extremism results between the different religions.

Why do you go to the worship services of your church, synagogue or mosque and make a monetary offering? Is it not that you believe this to be advantageous, that the minister, priest, rabbi, or imam, is an agent of God with special powers to prepare you for the Hereafter? If you do not believe, that the preaching's of religion are advantageous, why do you then attend your mosque, church or temple? The fact that you attend is a clear demonstration that you believe attendance, and making an offering will be advantageous in order to secure entry into the supernatural world.

Although belief in a supernatural world is not essential to life itself, such belief will be for some a source of comfort and solace in conducting one's life affairs. It, therefore, will be only when religion makes false claims and misleading statements, or creates its own laws contrary to logic, and common sense, or it defies society's laws, that it does a disservice in performing its role in society.

Religion as a Social Club

The sacred books of the different religions are great stories. The fact that billions of humans believe those stories is a testament to the importance religion plays in the lives of many humans. The fact that the sacred books of religion are great stories, and billions believe the stories, does not make those stories true. If there was one true story, there would be no need for the competition from the different religions for our offerings.

What the different stories and myths of religion do tell us, is that for many humans there is need to believe in a higher power, notwithstanding no one has yet found or seen this higher power. It is also a testament to the acumen of the different religious businesses in promoting their stories. Hero worship is a great preoccupation of humans, whether it be in religion, government, theater, sports, or other forms of endeavor. Like all things that bring pleasure to humans, fellowship in a common religious bond serves a similar feeling of pleasure and satisfaction.

Religion from the beginning of time has been a product of man's dreams of something greater than himself, a hope for a destiny beyond this world. Religion is the agency that has taken on the role of providing this hope for man. It has always had magical, supernatural elements. In modern times the symbols of the crucifix, the skull cap, prostrating oneself facing Mecca, or in the Islamic hajj throwing stones at two pillars, symbolizing the devil, are examples of devices used to signify the distinctiveness and special ness of one's religion. Our countryside-the cities, towns and villages of our world- is dotted with the various worshiping places of the different religions- an impressive testament to the importance of religion in the life of man.

The symbols, rituals and garments of primitive religions, we may view with curiosity and disbelief, but they are no different from the meanings attached to the symbols, rituals and different vestments and practices of the purveyors of modern day religion. Religion, if it operates as a special club, with a particular set of rituals and symbols, and a central mission can perform a valuable service to many in society. It is only when that club pretends that it is more than a club, and makes claims not borne out by the evidence, and seeks offerings under false pretences, and disobeys the laws of society, that society should be concerned.

One cannot be but uplifted and invigorated from attending one's church, or synagogue, or mosque, through the music, chanting, prayers, use of ritual, and the messages imparted to believers, including the social interaction that takes place. There are many non-religious organizations or societies, clubs, fraternities and cults that play a similar, and equally important role in our daily lives. Writers of books of fiction, and music; producers of theater, and movies, and popular entertainment satisfy a similar need of humans.

It may be just human nature for some believers to believe from all the symbols, ritual, vestments and ceremony of religion that their local priest or minister is actually an agent of God with special powers to prepare them for a Hereafter. The same leap of faith applies to some of the public in the belief of the power of those in government, and our judicial system, based upon the same ritual, vestments and ceremony. This only becomes harmful if it results in unfair practices, and atrocities committed in the name of religion, or government.

Religion, in its celebration of life's secular registration of births, marriage and death by providing a religious ceremony can be a more meaningful expression in the celebration of life's main events than filing the evidence to your local government office. Its work with the poor and sick, and its work on morals and ethics, can provide a valuable service to humans. Religion has flourished, not only because of its good works, but because the public believe that it does have power to prepare one for the Hereafter. One, in life, does not always act in rational ways. Make believe also has a place. Good people sometimes cross the line between fact and speculation, or make believe, because of misinformation, or lack of knowledge of the scientific evidence for evolution of the universe and man, and the lack of knowledge of the history for the evolution of modern day religion.

Those in religion for the most part are good people doing good works, even if they are promoting a myth or story in seeking offerings to secure the energy of life, and all of life's other amenities. All they have to do is honour the following commandment. Doing so, they would enhance their role in society:

"You shall not bear false witness against your neighbour"
(Exodus 20:16).

I have no problem with religion as speculation and make believe. My problem for Christianity is when clerics only tell part of the story and do not disclose information from report of its own Christian scholars on the gospels as myth and stories, that the virgin birth of Jesus, is a theological statement, and not a biological statement, and that Jesus probably died as do all other humans.Ignoring the evidence from science and evidence from Christian scholars, religious clerics who seek offerings from believers, become subject to the allegation of seeking offerings under false pretences or fraudulently.

I recognize that Christian clerics are in a conflict of interest, for if they tell the whole story, they would be concerned that offerings may no longer flow, and their businesses may fail. However, failing to tell the whole story in the seeking of offerings from believers is tantamount to a criminal finding of fraudulent behavior, in seeking offerings from believers under false pretenses.(Criminal Code of Canada, Part IX-Offences and Rights and Property, s. 365.) Democratic governments that provide tax relief for religious offerings, and that recognize religion in the public sphere as a legitimate authority, would be subject to a finding of being guilty of aiding and abetting that fraudulent behavior.

To ensure that Christianity is fully transparent and accountable to believers, and to avoid an allegation of fraudulent behavior, Christianity needs to clearly provide information in one religious service annually by an independent source the findings to believers of science and its Christian scholars.

SERMON ON THE MOUNT

The business plan of all religions has been founded upon an unknown-the existence of a God. Religion's proof of the existence of God is its revelation, or sacred book. It is from each religion's sacred book, that each have developed their institutional structure - sacraments, ritual and ceremony on the pretense that they have insider knowledge on God's wishes, and are God's agents with the necessary skills and expertise to prepare man for the Hereafter. The business plans of all religions capitalize on our fear of death, and desire for eternal life. Many believers accept the messages of their religion, as their will to believe is so great. The only cost is occasional offerings in support of a particular religion's business plan. However, the human cost becomes much greater, when as true believers, religious fanaticism results in the competition for offerings, and governments fail to hold religions accountable for their atrocities. When governments provide legitimacy to religion in the place it gives religion in the conduct of government, the government must share responsibility for those atrocities.

Like many of you, I was born into a religion. In my case, it was as a Presbyterian. I had no choice, but accepted my parent's choice. When one grows up in a religion, it is difficult to contemplate, that some of the messages of religion may not be true. It becomes very difficult, after years of indoctrination, through sermons, hymns, prayers, music, and so on, to think otherwise. This only becomes negative, when speculation is promoted as fact. Such indoctrination becomes more serious when the State funds religion, as the State, then, becomes an agent of indoctrination, which should be a concern to members of all faiths, whether they be Christian, Judaic, Islamic, or the thousands of other religious sects, as indoctrination is antithetical to the concept of a liberal education, where the State provides the knowledge, and leaves the student to arrive at his or her own conclusions based upon that knowledge. (Appendix C)

Most of those engaged in religion are good people, who believe that they can save you, or me, and the world. They may be misguided, but their idealism can be a positive force in society. We all need some make-believe in our lives, and religion serves that purpose. Where religion has a problem, is when it crosses the line between speculation and fact, for example- the Bible is the word of God, rather than the words of men, inspired by a Holy Spirit, or when a priest, or minister, or rabbi, or imam creates the impression in a blessing of a building, or person, that he or she is an agent of God, with special powers, or when he or she pretends to have insider knowledge on morals and ethics, and makes statements that God wants you to do this,or that.

We all should search for the truth, and decide for ourselves, by considering the merits of the evidence presented by all sides. This will be difficult for some, however, when confronted by evidence that contradicts, or questions their religion's evidence, when from birth they have only been provided evidence from their religion. It was about 170 years after the demise of Jesus that various writers put together the Bible as their business plan in seeking offerings. The Bible went under many revisions, and remained the secret domain of clerics until 1380's when John Wycliffe produced the first handwritten version.

With the invention of the printing press in 1450 the Christian Bible became available to all believers, and many versions of truth developed. If Christianity had kept the Bible secret we would not have so many versions of the truth. We would only have the Bible's version. But some brave believers demanded to see the Bible. Hence we have many versions of the truth. The Roman Catholic Church has its version. The Eastern Catholic Church (1050) has its version. With the Protestant Reformation (1517) we have many more versions of the truth. Jews have their version. Islam has its version.

I believe in the report of Christian religious scholars, and the evidence from science. I do not believe in the Bible as the word of God, the virgin birth, the divinity of Jesus, as the son of God, the existence of the angel

Gabriel, or a Holy Spirit (Dove and tongues of fire). I am agnostic on the existence of God. In other words, I do not know if there is a God that exists. But if there is a God, who exists, it will not be the God of Christianity, Islam, Judaism, or any of the other religions based upon a revelation from their God.

I do not believe that most clerics in Christianity and in the other religions to-day are purposely misrepresenting the facts. They may be misinformed on the history for the evolution of Christianity, or their religion, and science, or if informed, blind to the reality of the myths and stories of their religion. There is a segment of society, by its very nature, which is gullible to the advertising of all businesses, including the business of religion. There will always be some scam and fraud artists in any business, and religion also will have its examples.

With respect, what believers need to remember is that the Christian Bible was written by men about 2000 years ago, alleged to have been communicated by God through a Holy Spirit to the writers of the Bible. Christian scholars have acknowledged that the gospels were written by third generation authors on the basis of folk memories preserved in stories, which had circulated by word of mouth for decades. To believe in the Bible as the words of God, you would have to believe in angels and Holy Spirits (Luke, verses 26 to 35). I do not believe in angels, and Holy Spirits. The Torah and Koran, and all the other sacred and holy books were also written by men, based upon spirits, dreams, or visions. I believe that the words of men 2000 years ago, are no more sacred than the words of men to-day. I, therefore, reject much of the Bible as historical fact. The Bible may be a great book of literary content, but not fact. So when believers quote many of the passages from the Bible, as fact, I am not impressed. Alfred North Whitehead made the following comment on the death of knowledge:

"Not ignorance, but ignorance of ignorance is the death of knowledge."

Part 1: The Pillars of Christianity in seeking offerings from believers, hopefully will end some of that ignorance by providing believers a bare bones look at religion as a business. It is only when humans become more knowledgeable on the science for the evolution of the universe, and the history for the evolution of religion, that ignorance of ignorance and the death of knowledge will have ended. When ignorance of ignorance ends, the conflict, discrimination, and atrocities committed by the different religions in the modern world will also end.

It has not been easy for me to report. It has been difficult, after many years of attending Church, and being the recipient of my mother's Bible readings to realize that much of what I was taught, although well meaning, was untrue. It was only because of an inquiring mind, and being skeptical of anything, unless I was satisfied that it was supported by evidence, that I pursued my questioning. However, I recognize that as humans we do not live by facts alone. Stories and myths oftentimes provide meaning to our lives, and so long as those stories and myths do not lead to the pretense that those in religion, for example -are something that they are not, actual agents of God with special powers to forgive sin, and have insider knowledge on morals and ethics, those stories and myths can be a source of inspiration and comfort to many believers.

Will I be burned at the stake, as was Giordano Bruni who suggesting that there were planets and suns in the universe other than our Sun? Will I have to go into hiding as Salman Rushdie for his book "The Satanic Verses" for allegedly defaming Muhammad? Will the Roman Catholic Church re-instate the Index of Prohibited books to silence me? Or will Christians, and those of all the other religions become more enlightened from the information that I have provided on the nature of religion, as a business? If your religion does not disclose the information from science on the evolution of the universe and man, and for Christianity the report of its Christian Scholars, I recommend that believers withhold their offerings until such time as their religion becomes more transparent and accountable. I have no problem with religion, as speculation and make believe, but Christianity must obey its 9th Commandment:

"You shall not bear false witness against your neighbor" (Exodus 20:16)

All the other religions must also avoid in their messages, bearing false witness to their believers.

PART 11

PILLARS OF DEMOCRATIC GOVERNMENTS IN SEEKING THE PAYMENT OF TAXES FROM BELIEVERS

INTRODUCTION

The first laws in ancient times were made by authority figures and councils of elders. They performed their role with wisdom, often accompanied, or re-enforced by witchcraft- sorcery, crafty science and fortune telling. For religion the law was received in a revelation from a supernatural God. For government the law was received in a revelation from its temporal God - a president or prime minister, and sons of God, through the rules of legislative procedure. For the courts, the holy judgments (revelations) were delivered from God (judge) and sons of God (jurors) through the use of the rules of evidence. The common ground for religion, government and the courts would be moral and ethical behavior. For religion, obeying God's law becomes necessary to gain entry into the supernatural world, and for the law of the government, and the courts, as the arbiters of the government's law, adherence to the secular law would become necessary to live the good life in the real world.

The religious authority often vied with the temporal authority for supremacy in servicing the needs of man. Sometimes both the religious authority and temporal authority resided in one authority. However, for democratic countries in modern times, although they pretend that the religious authority and temporal authority are separate, in reality, the religious authority has been a major force, often in opposition to the temporal authority.

The religious and temporal authorities competing for the allegiance of believers, each developed their own law. For religion, the religious law is found in their sacred books. For democratic governments, the secular law is found in the government's Bible (constitution) and the criminal, civil laws, and regulations of government, inspired by the secular God, and the sons of God, and revealed to believers by the secular Gods (judges) and sons of God (jurors) of their Courts. For religion's God, his, or her agents on Earth became the promoters of the religious law in the real world, in preparation for judgment day in the supernatural world. For the courts of democratic governments, the God (judges) and sons of God (jurors) of the courts become the arbiters and the judges of the government's law in the real world.

How did the businesses of religion begin? All forms of life, including man require the food energy created by the photosynthesis of light received from our Sun. To secure this necessary food energy, religion created its Hereafter Business. In its business plan, it would sell the service of preparation of man for an everlasting life in a Hereafter. For this service religion would seek offerings from its believers. Those offerings would support its business, and for believers would be necessary to gain entry into the Hereafter.

Religion would use its offerings to provide the infrastructure (places of worship) and underwrite the costs of its services, including the costs for the personal shelter and necessities of life for its underlings. From this central goal Judaism, Christianity, Islam, Ba'hai, and a multitude of other sects evolved seeking offerings to secure the food energy necessary for life- all competing for offerings from believers.

The business of government evolved in a similar manner as religion. To secure the food energy created by our Sun, and the shelter, and all the other necessities for life, conservatives and liberals, republicans and democrats compete for the favor of believers in seeking to be the government. Conservatives and liberals, republicans and democrats would use many of the same pillars as Christianity to convince believers that their President or Prime Minister is God and that members of parliament or congress are the sons of God, who serve the public's interest.

In its earliest form in Athens, with its small population base, all the people had a direct say in the operation of government in determining the laws and actions of the City State. This became known as democracy.

Later, with larger populations, as it became impossible to provide the input of all individual citizens in determining the laws, and actions of the State, each person's vote no longer became a direct vote on the affairs of the State, but only counted in deciding which person would directly represent believers in determining the laws and actions of the State.

Western governments soon began the process of convincing believers that this later development of casting a vote for a person, other than for yourself, that he or she would be representing your interest, when in reality, through the crafty science of democracy, in effect, it only resulted in electing an oligarchy, a government by the few, who may, or may not represent your interest. For the taxes you pay to the government, the government would pass the necessary laws, and the courts would provide the necessary services, to ensure that justice was received based upon the government's law. For the taxes you pay to the government, if you obey the secular laws, you will receive heaven on Earth. For your offerings to religion, if you obey God's laws, you will gain entry into the Hereafter in the supernatural world.

The business plan for democratic governments would be to provide for believers Heaven on Earth. Governments would provide the necessary infrastructure for the good secular life- hospitals, fire stations, police stations, roads, railways, airports, and related services, as found in the different national, state, provincial, and local levels of government. For this infrastructure, and service the government would not seek voluntary offerings, or need to resort to begging as does religion, but would require believers to pay taxes to cover the costs of the government's infrastructure and services. God and the sons of God of democratic governments would use the crafty science of democracy as justification for the payment of taxes, pretending that when believers vote for members of government, that the payment of taxes was approved by the people.

Whereas the revelation(Bible) for religion is eternal and unchanging, not tied to place and time, the revelation (constitution) in the prayer book for the government, upon which the laws of the government, and rulings of the courts is based, is tied to place and time, is relative, and is not eternal. Whereas religion promises that if you make offerings to your religion that you will be saved in a Hereafter, the Prayer Book of the government promises that if you pay taxes to your government, you will be provided with Heaven on Earth.

Whereas for Christianity,the revelation of the Bible was written by men about two thousand (2,000 years ago), inspired by a Holy spirit from the supernatural God, the revelations (constitutions) for democratic governments, in particular, Canada (147 years ago) United States (257 years ago) were written by men inspired by the rules of legislative procedure.

Whereas the goal of the business plan of religions is to provide the infrastructure and those services necessary in the real world to prepare man for heaven in a supernatural world, the goal of the business plans of democratic governments and their courts is to provide the infrastructure, and those services necessary, such as - health care, police protection, and justice to provide heaven in the real world.

Whereas the morals and ethics of Christianity (Ten Commandments, Beatitudes and Virtues), were alleged to have been received from God through a Holy Spirit, and Judgement Day would occur in the supernatural world, the revelations (criminal and civil laws) of democratic governments needed no inspiration from a Holy Spirit, but were created by men using the rules of legislative procedure, and justice for the democratic courts was created by men using the rules of evidence, and the courts revelations (holy judgements) delivered by the secular God (judge), and sons of God (Jurors) in the real world.

Whereas Christianity's God is in three persons- the father, the son, and the Holy Ghost, the secular Gods of democratic governments are the father (President or Prime Minister) and the sons of God (members of the House of Commons, or Congress, and Senate), and for the Courts, the father, being the judge, and the sons of God, members of a jury.

For Christianity, witchcraft or crafty science is when as non-scientists, the early writers of the Bible make the statements that God created the universe, and the first man and woman were Adam and Eve, and that Jesus is the son of God. Telling fortunes fraudulently is when

Christian clerics seek offerings from believers for consideration (money) promoting that if you are good, you will be saved in a Hereafter, but provide no proof of a Hereafter. Sorcery (magic, ritual and ceremony) is to create the pretence that Christian clerics are agents of God.

For western governments this same witchcraft is found in the crafty science of democracy to convince believers that God, and the sons of God of democratic governments, represent the people. The telling of fortunes fraudulently is when democratic government's promise goodies before an election, and fail to deliver. Sorcery is in the use of magic, ritual, and ceremony by democratic governments to convince believers that their President or Prime Minister is God, and that members of congress or parliament are the sons of God.

My objective, as for religion, is also to save the world. The world can only be saved if believers separate fact from faith, that the secular God, and sons of God of individual democratic governments are the greatest Gods, and sons of God in the world, otherwise the conflict and atrocities committed in the name of individual democratic governments will continue.

For democratic governments five foundation pillars, based upon faith, are used in seeking the payment of taxes from believers to secure the energy for life. Those five foundation pillars of democratic governments are supported by three marketing pillars:

THE FIVE FOUNDATION PILLARS OF DEMOCRATIC GOVERNMENTS

1. The Pillar of Faith in the Existence of God (Prime Minister or President)

The existence of the Christian God is an article of faith, I quote:

> **God: "The existence of God is an article of faith, clearly communicated in divine Revelation. The infinitely perfect Supreme Being uncaused and absolutely self-sufficient, eternal, the Creator and end of all things. The one God subsists in three equal persons, the Father and the Son, and the Holy Spirit.** (The 2010 Roman Catholic Almanac, Bunson, P 143)

For Christianity faith is the norm or standard of religious belief. I quote:

> **Rule of Faith: The norm or standard of religious belief. The Catholic doctrine is that belief must be professed in the divinely revealed truths in the Bible and tradition, as interpreted and proposed by the infallible teaching authority of the Church.** (Bunson, P. 141)

The Bible, written by men, inspired by the Holy Spirit, is alleged to contain divine revelation constituting the rule of faith. I quote:

> **"The canon of the Bible is the Church's official list of sacred writings. These works, written by men under the**

inspiration of the Holy Spirit, contain divine revelation and, in conjunction with tradition and teaching authority of the Church, constitute the rule of the Catholic faith (Bunson, P. 96)

The existence of the all powerful, all perfect, all knowing Gods of democratic government oligarchies, in disguise as democracies, is not a mystery, and needs no faith or Holy Spirit for belief in his or her existence. He or she may be a President or Prime Minister, who may be elected by his or her political party, or the people, and who serves on behalf of his or her political party, or the people through the crafty science of democracy. Believers actually see God, and see how through the rules of legislative procedure he created Canada, the United States of America, the United Kingdom, and all the other democratic countries in the world. Seeing is believing!!!

Whereas the God of religion is unchanging, eternal, and uncaused, the Gods of democratic governments are not unchanging, and not eternal, but caused through the use of the crafty science of democracy, and serve at the whim and fancy of the people. Whereas the supernatural God of religion is not accountable for floods, earthquakes, disease and natural disasters, the Gods of democratic governments are accountable. If the God of a democratic government fails to be accountable he or she may be replaced by his or her political party, or the people.

The pillar of faith is necessary for believers to accept the existence and power of the Gods of religion. Each religion believes that it is the true religion of God. In the same fashion, each country, relying on the pillar of faith believes that it is the true country of its secular God. Whereas the Gods of religion use the threat of divine intervention to protect their interests, the supreme Gods of democratic governments uses the power of executive privilege to protect their interests.

2. The Pillar of Faith That Members of Parliament or Congress Are the Sons of God

The God of Christianity is in three persons-God, the son of God, and the Holy Spirit. I quote, in part:

> **Holy Spirit: God the Holy Spirit, third Person of the Holy Trinity, who proceeds from the Father and the Son, and with him, he is equal and every respect ; inspirer of the prophets and writers of Sacred Scripture; appeared in the form of a dove at the baptism of Christ and as tongues of fire at his descent upon the Apostles ; soul of the Church and guarantor, by his abiding presence and action, of truth in doctrine--.** (Bunson, P. 144)

The Gods for democratic governments are not created in three persons, but in many persons. They need no holy spirit for their creation. The Gods, and sons of God- members of parliament or congress, are created by the people through the crafty science of democracy.

3. The Pillar of Faith That Through the Crafty Science of Democracy, God and the Sons of God, Will Represent the People.

In democratic governments founded on the crafty science of democracy, it is claimed that the people hold the power. As you can only represent the people in a direct democracy, where every person has a vote on every issue, which is not possible in modern times, because of our vast populations, the religious pillar of faith becomes important to re-enforce the belief that the democratic God represents the people.

Why does God, and the sons of God in government claim that when you vote in a democracy, this means that the government is representing the people? If believers believe that God, and the sons of God represent the people, the government's law would become enforceable by the government's police and courts, unlike religion, where its law is enforceable only on judgment day in the supernatural world. If believers believe that God and the sons of God of democratic governments represent the people, believers will pay taxes to democratic governments, and the God and sons of God of democratic governments will use the taxes to secure their energy for life, and will in turn provide the services and infrastructure necessary for heaven on Earth for believers.

Whereas the work of religion is to separate what is good, from what is evil in the real world, and promote what is good in the real world in order for believers to gain entry into a make-believe, unknown supernatural world, the work of God,and the sons of God of democratic governments in the real world is to separate what is good, from what is evil, in order to create the laws necessary to live the good life in the real world. Whereas for religions, the way to Heaven is participation in each religion's sacraments, and the making of regular offerings, the way to Heaven on Earth for democratic governments, is participation in the crafty science of democracy, and the payment of taxes by believers.

How does God, and the sons of God of democratic governments convince believers that they will provide Heaven on Earth? They use political parties. What is a political party? It is a group of people, whose common interest is usually of two different kinds- reducing the role of government, so that individual autonomy is enhanced, or increasing the role of government, so that individual welfare is advanced. Those of the first kind are usually called conservatives or republicans, and those of the second kind, liberals or democrats, although any party, whether called Conservative, Liberal, Republican or Democrat, or any other such name, will have some members of the view of the other kind.

The different interests, within parties are not unlike the different interests within religions. In Judaism, there is orthodox, reformed and conservative. In Christianity there is Eastern Orthodox, Roman Catholic, and Protestant. Within Protestant, there is Presbyterian, United, Baptist, Lutheran, Anglican, and so on. Within Islam there are the Shia and Sunni and many other sects - all with different views of reality in the universe.

Webster's New Third International Dictionary, 1961, defines conservative as follows:

> **"the disposition in politics to reserve what is established; a political philosophy based on a strong sense of tradition, and social stability, stressing the importance of established institutions (religion, property, the family, and class structure) and preferring gradual development with preservation of the best elements of the past to abrupt change; the tendency to accept an existing fact, order,**

situation, or phenomenon, and to be cautious toward or suspicious of change; extreme wariness and caution in outlook, which normally increases with age and sagacity."

Conservatives are those who resist change. They worship the past. They lack creativity. They cannot think out of the box. They have a high opinion of themselves. They believe that they are acting on behalf of a higher power. They find it difficult to compromise, or to accept that there is another valid point of view on an issue.

Webster's New Third International Dictionary, 1961, defines liberal as follows:

"Marked by generosity, bounteousness, openhandedness; not confined or restricted to exact or the literal; not narrow in mind; not bound by authoritarianism or orthodoxy, or traditional or established forms in action, attitude or opinion.; a man~ of views who would not mind making significant changes in the social or economic structure if he felt it were for the best; the most general term suggests an emancipation from convention, tradition or dogma that extends from a belief in altering institutions to fit altering conditions to a preference for lawlessness; on the one hand it suggests a commendable pragmatism, tolerance and broad mindedness, and on the other a highly questionable unorthodoxy, experimentalism,, or positive irresponsibility; social legislation to benefit the masses and to break the power of the privileged; an adherent or advocate of liberalism especially in terms of individual rights and freedom from arbitrary authority."

Liberals or democrats are those who defy convention, participate in marches, wave signs, question existing practices, and are generally considered as nuisances by the establishment. If they saw their shadow they would run. It is liberalism, however, that promotes change, and advances progress. Without liberal thinkers, slavery would be current, and women would continue to be denied the right to vote.

Most advances result from liberal thinking, but liberalism is not the sole preserve of Liberals or Democrats. Advances can sometimes be generated by Conservatives or Republicans. The accepted liberal measures of to-day, become the conservative tradition of to-morrow, that conservatives will to-morrow fight to preserve, and liberals to change. And so change, and progress, however it is defined, goes on.

Is it important to know whether your candidate is conservative or liberal, democrat or republican? Certainly on many issues it is, if you have a particular view on abortion, same sex marriage, contraception, and so on, and want to advance your cause. This raises the question, is there any practice or issue so sacred, and eternal, that consideration of change, is not up for debate. The very religious believe that there is, but are unable to secure agreement on what is eternal, and unchanging or absolute about any of their laws, virtues, or causes. They refer to God for counsel, but since they are unable to explain how they are able to communicate with their God, they instead pretend to be God. Non-believers, as a result, are not convinced of any of their pronouncements.

Political parties promise all kind of goodies, if you vote for their candidates. They offer improvements in health care, reductions in taxation, and new or improved social services, if you vote for their political party. Why do they engage in fortune telling of goodies, if elected? They want the rewards and all the perks that go with being the government- gold plated pensions, personal aides, prestige, security, limousines,air travel fitting their rank, and the ability to make patronage appointments to their friends, and reward their benefactors.

To maintain power, the main task for a political party is discipline of its members- ensuring that all members of the party have the same view on any issue, or are singing from the same hymn book. The main task of the opposing party is to take the opposite point of view or position. To agree to the position of the other party is considered sacrilege. In breaking ranks with the party, and or Prime Minister or President on an issue is considered ignoble. The nature of party structures may be great at focusing on priorities, but when opposition to the opposing party becomes more important, than making the right decision, parties provide a disservice to believers.

An important task of parties is to raise money in order to promote their agendas. This is done through the crafty science of marketing where governments resort to bribery to seek offerings from believers by offering a tax credit for a portion of a believer's political contributions to be eligible for a tax reduction. For the prospective donor, in a democracy, such credits are considered as a down payment on entry into heaven on Earth. Governments also provide religions with a tax credit for a portion of an individual's contributions to his church, synagogue or mosque, to be eligible for a tax reduction. For governments this is known as covering your ass in the event that the speculation and make believe of religion is true. Religious believers use the tax credit of government to defray the cost of their offerings, or payments necessary in gaining entry into the Hereafter.

To become the candidate for your party you must first of all have the approval of electors in your riding or jurisdiction, at a special meeting called for that purpose, known as a nomination meeting, or primary. For some parties, and for some ridings, or congressional districts finding a candidate is difficult. Much arm twisting is required. The party must have a candidate. Qualifications of the candidate, position on issues, and the like, are irrelevant.

In some other ridings, or jurisdictions the opposite is true. There is great interest in being a candidate, particularly if the candidate, once selected by his party, is in a riding or district favorable to the party, and the likelihood of election is great. In such circumstances the main contest is becoming the representative of the party, as winning the election is assured. As a result, much conivery is employed - revision of the rules, changing of deadlines, and all sorts of such shenanigans by candidates, and their handlers to secure the desired result of being nominated as the candidate.

Who are they who seek office through the crafty science of democracy? Whereas in religion, the major qualification is faith in God to be a member of a religion, the major qualifications to be members of government are: big ego, rich, unemployed, a forked tongue, ability to engage in double talk, and the ability to spin any issue, in such a manner, as to persuade you, that they are representing your interests - also known as representing the people.

Candidates for office also need offerings from their believers, as do clerics in religion to support their life on Earth. They engage in debates with their opponents- kiss babies, shake hands, say things that they do not believe, knock on doors, seek donations to their cause, and drink lots of coffee. You know when a politician is in trouble by the number of times he uses the words- that he or she seeks to represent the people. Important phrases used are - the fact of the matter is; we are moving forward; we support freedom and liberty. Their main interest, once elected, however, will not be your interest, but their self -interest of becoming re-elected.

How does a member of the public decide which candidate is the most worthy of his or her vote? Electors come in many forms- ignorant of the issues, their mind already made up, not interested, interested, but will only support a candidate, if promised a reward. If a member of the public decides to vote, and a significant number do not bother, how does a member of the public decide for whom to cast his vote? He must rely upon the pillar of faith, as most members of the public have little knowledge of a candidate's qualifications, or position on the different issues. As a result, all the factors having no relationship to the merits of the candidate come into play - the candidate's religion, ethnicity, language, color, gender and width of his or her smile.

The numerals of mathematics form the basis for the crafty science of democracy. Decisions in a democracy are passed by the simple process of counting. In parliament or congress members yell back and forth across the aisle, when in great excitement about particular issues of the day, bow before the speaker of the House, clap their hands when a member of their party scores a blow over the opposition, mouth their name, or yell aye or nay, when called upon to vote. If those on the other side of the aisle, or members opposite, can count higher, than your side of the aisle, then the members opposite, or the other side of the aisle wins.

Counting becomes a periodic ritual in democratic countries to create the impression that your elected representative is representing the people. To re-enforce this belief, ballots are printed with names of the candidates, where you gamble, as if in a lottery, as to which candidate is most worthy of your vote. To further foster this belief you must hide or conceal yourself in a special place, and secretly place an X beside the name of a particular candidate. In a democracy, the candidate with the greatest number of X's beside his or her name becomes a son of God, who pretends to represent the people.

How can a prospective candidate represent you, if you have never met the candidate, or have any knowledge of his or her views on the issues, other than general matters of the moment? And what if you cast your vote, and the candidate for whom you did not cast your vote, wins? What happens, then? Obviously he or she does not represent you. It is the pillar of faith in the crafty science of democracy that is necessary to believe that if you cast a vote for a candidate, even if the candidate you voted for is not successful, that the candidate who is successful will be representing your interest.

But even if your candidate is successful, in reality, he or she can only represent himself or herself. How many times has the successful candidate you voted for consulted with you on any issue? The use of the term democracy, to convey the impression that a candidate is representing your interests, is therefore a fiction. It is only those who are successful in being elected, who are able to represent their interests, but only if they are part of the majority of votes on an issue. But even if one of the majority votes, because of party discipline, their vote may not be their own vote, but that of their leader.

But once elected, and forming the government, or forming the opposition, how much power has an elected member? Very little, unless a member is a member of the cabinet, or executive branch, as back benchers often do not have direct input into the government's or opposition's agenda. Although there is provision for private member's bills, how many significant private members' bills have ever passed? Even being a member of the cabinet, you may be part of the minority on an issue. Cabinet ministers, or those members of the executive branch of government serve at the whim and fancy of the President or Prime Minister. Serving at the whim and fancy of the President or

Prime Minister, or any other such leader, where your position of power and influence including monetary rewards depends on approval of the leader, acts as a serious obstacle to freedom of expression, and severely limits the power of those members of the cabinet or executive who desire to take a different position from their leader.

The real influences on government policy will be the professional members of the bureaucracy who provide advice to the elected members. Those members of the bureaucracy are appointed through the crafty science of appointment, where often, it is not skill and knowledge that is important but the width of their smile, religion, race, gender or friendship that is the decisive factor. The skill and knowledge of members of cabinet or the executive will be particularly important, and subject to the same problems in appointment, as for the bureaucracy. Success in negotiations between a President or Prime Minister with their counter parts in other governments, including cabinet members with their counterparts in other governments, often will not be based upon skill and knowledge on an issue, but based upon personal qualities and attitudes of the parties.

In reality, western governments who worship democracy, are really oligarchies, disguised as democracies, as the crafty science of democracy is only a means for determining who are the small numbers of persons who represent your interest. The United States of America pretends to operate under the purest form of democracy, where even some judges are elected by the people, but it often acts as if it is a theocracy, when being a member of the Christian religion is believed, as being necessary to be president.

A candidate seeking election, as president, who does not secure the greatest number of votes, can still become president in the United states of America, as the president is determined not by who had the greatest number of votes in the nation, but who had the greatest number of electoral votes, where each state in the nation is allocated a predetermined number of votes in the electoral college. In a country of three hundred million plus people, only five hundred and forty-five persons are able to represent their interests, although their interests may be broadly the same as many of the public. And if only sixty percent of the three hundred million plus population votes, the five hundred and forty-five persons would only represent those sixty percent, leaving the remaining forty percent unrepresented. In a two party system, if the majority party has sixty percent of the seats of government, then only three hundred and twenty seven persons represent the people (three hundred million population). If one considers party loyalty and discipline, many of the votes of those three hundred and twenty-seven members would not be their votes, but the votes of their leaders. In reality only a fractional percent of the people would be represented in an oligarchy, in disguise as a democracy. In a presidential democratic system it would be possible that only one person's vote, that of the President, through a veto, or executive order, that would be represented.

Canada is also really an oligarchy, disguised as a democracy, as the crafty science of democracy is only a means for determining who are the small number of persons who represent your interest. Canada is also an autocracy as members of the senate are appointed by the Prime Minister. It is also a theocracy as it only publicly funds those religions in existence at time of confederation (Appendix C), and recognizes the supremacy of a supernatural God in its sacred constitution. In Canada with its multi party system, it is possible for a party to secure less than fifty percent of the popular vote to form the government, and a candidate with less than fifty percent of the vote to become a member of parliament. In Canada, if a party is elected with forty percent of the vote but only sixty percent of the people voted in the election, that party would only represent about twenty five percent of the people.

The United Kingdom is also really an oligarchy, disguised as a democracy, as the crafty science of democracy is only a means used for determining who are the members of the oligarchy or House of Commons. The United Kingdom also operates as both an autocracy and a theocracy, as the government appoints members from both religion and secular society to its upper chamber- the House of Lords, and its head of state is an unelected hereditary Queen, and the Anglican religion is the State religion.

When the size of the population to elect a member in electoral districts varies, in oligarchies, disguised as democracies, no one would have an equal vote in comparison to the votes of those in other electoral districts, unless the size of the population in those electoral districts is equal. Promoting that in an oligarchy, disguised as a democracy, an elected member represents the people is therefore an illusion. The real decision makers, because of party discipline, often are only the members of the cabinet or executive branch, and sometimes only the President or Prime Minister. Democracy, in reality, is simply a word used to disguise government by the few, or an oligarchy.

4. The Pillar of Faith, That Through the Rules of Legislative Procedure, God, and the Sons of God, Have Created the Country's Sacred Constitution (Bible)

Christianity, and all the other religions, needed no rules of legislative procedure to create their sacred books (Bibles). The Christian God, through the Holy Spirit, just communicated her wishes to men, who wrote the Bible pretending to be scientists, by making claims about how God created the universe, Adam and Eve, and how God was the cause of light, and night and day- claims not borne out by the scientific evidence. God's workers on Earth, then, simply used the Bible pretending that they have insider knowledge of God's laws, and that they are God's agents with special powers to prepare man for a Hereafter, by making such statements, as God wants you to do this, or to do that.

Democratic governments, unlike religion, need rules of legislative procedure to create their Bible (constitution). Democratic governments received their Bible through dreams and visions from the prospective sons of God of their political parties using the rules of legislative procedure -Great Britain in the Magna Carta in 1215, the United States in its constitution of 1776, and in Canada its constitution of 1867. The government's Bible, then, formed the basis for the creation of the government's laws, and provision of services to believers.

In modern times, in the operation of government, the majority political party uses the crafty science of polling to decide which dreams and visions are placed on the government's order paper of the day. If the dreams and visions survive the different special interest groups, and lobbyists, God, and the sons of God of democratic governments use the rules of legislative procedures to create the new laws, or everyday revelations of democratic governments.

Robert's Rules of Procedures is an example of such rules and procedures used by democratic governments to create new laws. Such rules and procedures for democratic governments would include the following: the need for a roll call of members present; necessity of a quorum, or specified number of members present, if a valid decision is to be made; procedure for laying on the table for debate; recognition by speaker, if a member is to speak on a motion; form of debate, amendments, amendments to amendments, voting, referral to standing committee; re-tabling to committee of the whole, size of majority vote, if motion considered sacred; filibustering or prolonging debate to express dissent if unable to defeat a motion; method or how voting is to be conducted, and how proceedings are to be recorded.

Readers who wish more information on Canada's legislative procedures are requested to refer to the web site www.parl.gc.ca, where the stages in the Canadian legislative process are listed. I quote, in part:

> **"In the Parliament of Canada, as in all legislative assemblies based on the British model, there is a clearly defined method for enacting legislation. A bill must go through a number of specific stages in the House of Commons and the Senate before it becomes law: notice of motion for leave to introduce and placement on *Order Paper*; preparation of a bill by a committee (where applicable); introduction and first reading; reference to a committee before second reading (where applicable); second reading and reference to a committee; consideration in committee; report stage; third reading (and passage); consideration and passage by the Senate; passage of Senate amendments by the Commons (where applicable); Royal Assent, and coming into force.**
>
> **All bills must go through the same stages of the legislative process, but they do not necessarily follow the same route. The process is complex, but a bill can become law only**

once the same text has been approved by both Houses of Parliament and received Royal Assent."

For the American legislative process readers are directed to <u>www.clerk.house.gov/</u>. I quote, in part:

"Legislation originates in several ways. The Constitution provides that the President "shall from time to time give to the Congress Information of the State of the Union, and recommend to their Consideration such Measures as he shall judge necessary and expedient..."

The President fulfills this duty either by personally addressing a joint session of the two Houses or by sending messages in writing to Congress, or to either body thereof, which are received and referred to the appropriate committees. The President usually presents or submits his annual message on the state of the Union shortly after the beginning of a session."

"Senate and House bills and joint resolutions, when passed by both Houses in identical form and approved by the President, become public or private law--public laws affect the Nation as a whole; private laws benefit only an individual or a class thereof. The procedure on each is identical, with the exception of joint resolutions proposing amendments to the Constitution of the United States, which under the Constitution must be passed in each House by a two-thirds vote of the Members present and voting, a quorum being present. They are not sent to the President for his approval but to the Administrator of the General Services Administration, who transmits them to the various States. Constitutional amendments are valid when ratified by at least three-fourths of the States."

God and the sons of God of democratic governments use the rules of legislative procedure aided by little pages, dressed as witches, who flit here and there, at the beckon call of their masters, whereas for

Christianity, God needed no little pages dressed as witches, or rules of legislative procedure to assist her, but instead God used the holy spirit to communicate her wishes to men, who then wrote the Bible containing God's laws.

Which is more believable or more creditable? The revelation (constitution) of government oligarchies, disguised as democracies, using the rules of legislative procedure in their houses of worship at the federal, state or provincial, and municipal levels, where the secular God, and sons of God seek the payment of taxes from believers to provide the infrastructure, such as- fire stations, police buildings, airports, water purification plants, defense departments, hospitals, post offices, and related services in the real world, or the revelation of the Christian Bible from God inspired by a Holy Spirit, where clerics seek offerings from believers in the real world, necessary for believers to be saved on judgment day in a supernatural world, in order to provide their infrastructure- houses of worship, hospitals, and services to believers?

5. Faith That Through Fortune Telling That the Government Will Provide Perfect Laws (Morals and Ethics) To Provide Heaven on Earth

As fortune tellers, those in religion, act as modern day medicine men and witchdoctors, tell fortunes fraudulently, when they proclaim, that if man makes an offering, and participates in religion's sacraments, he will attain everlasting life in Heaven, but provide no proof of a Hereafter. To enter this Hereafter, faith in God, Moses, Jesus, or Muhammad is required, including following the laws of their religion, and making sacrifices, in modern times, in the form of making offerings (money), to support their Hereafter Businesses.

Political parties do their fortune telling usually prior to an election. They use the crafty science of polling of public opinion, and use focus groups, as the basis for their fortune telling of the future. They promise all kinds of goodies, if you elect them to their houses of worship. Political parties of government tell fortunes fraudulently of a heaven on Earth, when they make promises, that if elected, that they will provide certain services or infrastructure, and when elected they do not fulfill their promises.

Like religion, democratic governments woo their believers through marketing, advertising and puffing through the print and visual media. Religions do so through weekly sermons in their houses of worship to foster belief in the power of their religious God, and the truth of her revelations. Governments, also, through its various public legislative sessions in its houses of worship, and through advertising, and public meetings, foster belief in the power of its secular God- a prime minister or president, and the sons of God (members of parliament or congress) on the benefit to be derived by believers from the government's revelations (laws, statutes and regulations), and services. Whereas Christianity has no enforcement arm for failure of believers to observe its laws, democratic governments created police forces to ensure that the secular laws are observed by believers, and courts to deal with infractions of the secular law by believers.

THE THREE MARKETING PILLARS
OF DEMOCRATIC GOVERNMENTS

1. The Pillar of Worship of Idols (former and Current Saints of Government)

For belief in the power of God and the truth of his or her revelation to be accepted by believers, whether it be the absolute laws of religion, or the relative laws of the government, worship of idols becomes important.

For religion, whereas the worship of idols takes the form of the worship of Moses, Muhammad, Jesus Christ, and for the Roman Catholic religion- many other saints and idols, for democratic governments the pillar of worship of idols takes the form of regular practice in the worshiping of their founding fathers. In Canada, they worship the fathers of confederation- Sir John A. MacDonald, Thomas D'Arcy McGee, and Sir Oliver Mowat. For the United States they worship George Washington, Thomas Jefferson, and James Madison. For the United Kingdom they worship Queens and Kings and Sir Robert Walpole (1721-1732) considered as the first Prime Minister. The worship of idols is also found in the different cultural, sporting, entertainment, musical, artistic, and other great events, or attractions to celebrate the achievement of the Gods in secular society.

2. The Pillar of Periodic Visits to One's Holy Places (Charlottetown, Westminster and Gettysburg)

Whereas for religion the pillar of periodic pilgrimages to one's holy places - visits to Jerusalem, Lourdes, Mecca or Medina, and Bethlehem becomes important in reinforcing belief in the religious Gods, and the truth of their revelations, for democratic governments the pillar of periodic pilgrimages to their holy places become visits to Westminster, Charlottetown, Boston (American Revolution) and Gettysburg (address by Abraham Lincoln on American independence) reinforcing belief in the power of the secular Gods, and sons of God, and the truth of their revelations.

3. The Pillar of Sorcery (Magic, Ritual, Pomp and Ceremony) to Convince Believers That Their President or Prime Minister Is God, and That Members of the House of Commons or Congress Are the Sons of God

Sorcery in religion takes the form of magic, ritual, fancy clothes, the use of symbols, and pomp and circumstance in the performance of duties to convince believers that those in religion are agents of God. The creation of different symbols, different days for worship, dress and practices, saints, and holy days to separate each religion from other religions, becomes critical in each religion's marketing plan to gain favor in the recruitment of new believers in order to increase their offering base.

Sorcery in government takes on similar forms of magic, as in religion, to convince believers that a president or prime minister is God, and members of parliament or congress, are the sons of God. Some of the official persons of government dress in distinctive colors, on particular days, such as- opening and closing of their house of worship. Sorcery for government is also seen in the use of symbols, such as- the crown and eagle, flags, national anthems, and images of a former or past president, or current Queen, or King on a country's coinage. Their holy days become Victoria Day, President's day, Independence Day, Canada Day and the many other sacred days to celebrate God and the sons of God, and the saints of democratic governments.

The singing of the national anthems for democratic governments serves the same purpose in the indoctrination of believers, as does the recitation of the Lord's Prayer for believers in Christianity. It is the use of sorcery that makes each religion special, the true religion of God, in the competition for believers, that incites all the atrocities committed in the name of religion, as does sorcery for democratic governments in the competition for believers, through the use of flags, symbols, anthems, and oaths of allegiance, that incites wars against other countries or nation states, promoting that their country is the true and greatest nation in the world. The armies and police of democratic governments use the same magic, sorcery and ceremony to celebrate great victories, or other great events or sacrifices in the performance of their duties.

It is the political party for democratic governments, which is the best fortune teller, which usually wins the election using the crafty science of democracy. It is because of fortune telling that believers are willing to make sacrifices in the payment of taxes to secure heaven on Earth, as fortune telling is used in religion to convince believers that making of offerings will gain entry into Heaven in the supernatural world.

To convince believers in the power of the secular God and sons of God, special honors are provided by the secular God and sons of God to the government's citizens for valor, service, or accomplishment- Queen's Jubilee medal, Order of Canada, Knighthood, Citizen of the year, Congressional medal of Honor, Victoria Cross, Honorary citizens of the United States, Order of the Garter, and Order of the British Empire and addressed as Sir. Those in executive or cabinet positions in Canada and Great Britain are to be addressed as the Honorable to recognize their relative importance in relation to other members of government and society.

WHAT IF A CHRISTIAN GOVERNMENT?

But you ask, if our present democratic governments, and our courts operate under many of the same elements of witchcraft, and pillars as does Christianity, and western government oligarchies, disguised as democracies, only represents the opinion of those elected, and often only of the executive branch of government, and sometimes only of the Prime Minister or President, and does not represent all the people, and justice in our courts is an illusion, would the work of the government, and the courts be better served if they were replaced with a Christian government and its courts? What would a benevolent autocratic Christian government and its courts, operating as a theocracy look like?

It would replace the government's current coat of arms or eagle or sacred seal by a crucifix- the symbol of its leader. All judges of the Supreme Court would be required to be Christian clerics. The parliaments or congresses of Christian governments would consist of two main parties-the Roman Catholic and Protestant parties. We would replace our present constitution by the Bible. Our law would be based upon the Ten Commandments, the Beatitudes, and the Christian virtues. We would rely upon faith in Jesus. Members would recite the Lord's Prayer at the beginning of each parliamentary session, as homage to their leader. Since the work of our parliament or congress is based upon Christian fundamentals, and many in the world do not belong to the Christian party, we could consider re-establishing the Inquisition and Crusades, practiced many centuries ago by our Christian forefathers, and outlaw Judaism and Islam.

As the Christian sacred book of the Bible contains absolute truth in religious law, as communicated by God, through the angel Gabriel, and holy spirit, whereas the truth of the secular law of the government is contained in the government's revelation of the constitution, statutes, and the rulings of the courts is relative, and different for every jurisdiction, we would no longer need the secular courts, if we had a benevolent autocratic Christian government, as the law would be eternal and unchanging, and the penalties and rewards under the law would known, justice would be swift and certain.

We would no longer require elections if a Christian theocracy. Members of parliament or congress, and the courts would be appointed by God, and the son of God, and their agents- a Pope, or other supreme Christian leader. Decisions would be made by your local priest or minister. In a theocracy, operating as an autocracy, decision making would be swift and unencumbered by reason, as decisions would be made by a superior power, or by agents of that superior power, who would have divine wisdom.

Replacing our present secular justices of the Supreme Court by Christian justices would ensure that divine and absolute truth is followed. As a result we would be assured that marriage would be between a man and a woman, a woman's right to choose an abortion denied, and the prohibition against the sale of liquor would be re-instated.

We would no longer require taxation in a theocracy. Our churches, synagogues and mosques would seek offerings to support the theocracy, based upon the threat of not being saved. We would no longer require lawyers to protect us from violations of the law. They would be replaced by the religious medicine men and witch doctors - priests and ministers in the administration of justice for the religious law. The penalties and rewards would not occur in the real world, but be delayed until judgment day in the supernatural world.

Belief in the power of God, reliance upon faith that God exists, pretense to have insider knowledge on morals and ethics, and that those in religion are agents of God would be the cornerstones of a theocratic government, and marketed through sorcery, in the use of magic, ritual and ceremony. Through the study of the religious saints and idols, regular sessions would be held on the importance of the religious law.

We would make annual pilgrimages to Bethlehem and Jerusalem. These are some of the benefits to believers, if we replaced our present western government oligarchies, using the crafty science of democracy, disguised as democracies, by a Christian government, operating as a theocracy.

You likely think that I am making fun of replacing our government oligarchies, in disguise as democracies, with a theocratic Christian government operating as a benevolent autocracy. How dare you question my motives!! This is no laughing matter. If my assumption that electors in a democracy are generally ill- informed on the issues, and those who run for office are often ill-prepared to represent the ill-informed electorate, and the elements in the dynamics of the decision making process of democratic governments is not a guarantee that the correct decisions are made, decisions made by democratic institutions, will often be flawed, and therefore the belief that in a democracy, decisions made by the legislative branch are sacred will be a fiction,and may be no better than the decisions of a government operating as a Christian theocracy under the inspiration of the Holy Spirit.

The question that the reader must answer, is which of the two competing revelations has the greater legitimacy? The Christian revelation, unchanging and eternal in the form of the Bible, based upon words of men two thousand years ago, alleged to have been received from God through a Holy Spirit, or the changing and evolving revelations created by men to-day using the rules of legislative procedure in western government oligarchies, in disguise as democracies, pretending to represent the people?

PART 111

THE PILLARS OF DEMOCRATIC GOVERNMENT COURTS IN PROVIDING JUSTICE FOR BELIEVERS

INTRODUCTION

Because of the imperfections in the democratic process, and the sometimes less than perfect decisions made by their legislative branches, judicial review by the Courts provide the necessary interplay between democratic governments, and their courts, so that the decisions by the legislative branch can properly respect accepted Court wisdom, whether that be in accordance with the Court, or in the final analysis the decision of the legislative branch, based upon the Court's input. The judicial branch of government in such cases, will be a major check on the tyranny of democratic government oligarchies, disguised as democracies, pretending to represent the people.

The secular God, and sons of God of government express great concern that the Gods of the judicial branch of democratic governments, in its interpretations of the government's law, will actually revise the meaning of the government's revelations (statutes), and make the law. As a consequence, in appointment of the judges, or the worldly Gods of the Supreme Court, much hand wringing and chagrin is registered, about those persons who they feel may be activists conservative or liberal judges- judges that dare to challenge the wisdom of the representatives of the people.

Whereas the laws of religion are made to ensure that believers exhibit conduct pleasing to the supernatural God, the laws of government are made to ensure that the behavior of believers, in their relations among the other members of society, is pleasing to the secular God, and sons of God. For democratic governments it is the federal, state or provincial courts, which enforce infractions of the laws by believers. It is the Courts, that determine justice by acting as the arbiter in disputes about the law, whether the law be that of the constitution, or statutes passed by a government's legislature. The decisions of the Courts become the common law or the new revelations of the Courts, which may be cited in support of, or in opposition to, a legal argument. Some believe that the courts in applying or interpreting the law, also make the law.

Democratic governments use both the crafty science of democracy, and autocracy through appointment to create the Gods (judges) of the courts. The judges of the courts, where necessary, appoint the sons of Gods (jurors) on advice of the defence and prosecution. The Courts use many of the same elements of witchcraft, as does religion, relying upon faith, to create the impression that judges are God, and that the members of juries are the sons of God, with insider knowledge on morals and ethics, who can fortune tell the correct rewards and penalties that should be levied for infractions of the law.

Do the courts do any better job, acting as the judges and arbiters of the government's law, than the government in creating the law? Will the decisions of the courts be any wiser, than the decisions of democratic governments in creating the laws? To answer that question we will look at the pillars of the Courts.

THE FOUR FOUNDATION PILLARS OF DEMOCRATIC GOVERNMENT COURTS

1. The Pillar of Faith in the Existence of God (Judge)

Whereas the God of Christianity is unknown, and the son of God for Christianity is known, but unseen, the Gods (Judges) of the courts are known, and seen, and the sons of God (jurors) of the courts are also known, and seen. There is no mystery. The Gods of the courts are created by appointment, and in some States in the United States created by the crafty science of democracy. If appointed, they are created by the secular God, and sometimes the sons of God of democratic governments, and sometimes upon recommendations of their peers.

The Supreme God of the courts, is known as the Chief Justice, supported by a gaggle of mini sons of God, known as justices, not unlike the God of democratic governments- a President or Prime Minister, is supported by a gaggle of mini-Gods, or sons of God, known as members of parliament or congress. This is not unlike the Supreme God of Christianity supported by Jesus, the son of God, and for the Roman Catholic Church, a Pope, as the grandson of God, supported by a flank of The impressive worshiping places of the Courts are like the impressive seats or worshiping places of government, and the impressive worshiping places of churches, mosques and synagogues of religion. Lawyers, become the lackeys or handmaidens of the Courts, whereas for the laws of religion, the priests, ministers, rabbis or imams of the various branches of religion become the lackeys and handmaidens of the Gods of religion.

2. The Pillar of Faith in the existence of the sons of God (jurors)

The sons of God (jurors) for the courts are not elected, as the sons of God for parliament or congress are, but are appointed by the Gods of the courts (judges) from a random sample of qualified persons, where the defense and prosecution are permitted a specific number of challenges as to fitness to serve. In determining fitness to serve the defense and prosecution seek to find a juror who may be favorable to their position. Often consultants are hired to assist both the defense and prosecution in assessing as to whether a potential juror would be favorable to their client. The God of the court (judge) will make the final decision, if no agreement between the litigants.

3. The Pillar of Faith that God (Judge) and the sons of God (jurors) will receive truth through the Court's Rules of Evidence.

Believers are reminded that most laws in society are civil or regulatory, and not criminal. I quote from article of W. Vincent Clifford in the Ottawa Citizen of January 19, 2013 titled **"How the law rules all that we do"**, where he notes that in a country there are more regulatory offences than criminal, for example- in Canada there are more than 100,000 regulatory, as compared to 849 sections in the criminal code.

In a criminal proceeding, applying the rules of evidence becomes a game between the Prosecution and the Defense. Judges are the referees or umpires in this game. Victims seek revenge, the accused in escaping justice, the police and the prosecution in getting their man, and the defense escaping the application of the law. Every trick known to humans is used to achieve each of their goals. The greatest sin is lying under oath (hand on the Bible or other sacred book), known as perjury, and subject to penalty of the Court. Otherwise lying in court, as in religion is okay, unless you are caught. This game is called seeking justice.

For religion, truth is received from God, as found in religion's sacred books and needs no rules of evidence for its creation. For Christianity it was communicated to men two thousand years ago by a holy spirit. For the courts of democratic governments truth can only be received in a trial using the rules of evidence, and the rules for the admissibility of the evidence. The rules of evidence will vary from country to country, and within countries from state to state, or from province to province, resulting in justice having a different meaning depending upon the jurisdiction, and wisdom of the judges and juries.

Words such as the following would have specific meaning in a legal proceeding determining guilt or innocence: action, subpoena, summons, warrant, serve, pardon, parole, probation, custody, disposition, disclosure, due diligence, contempt, caution, concurrent sentence, allege, burden of proof, battery, bail, arraignment, necessity, hearsay, indictment, habeas corpus, summons, privileges, witnesses, opinion, expert testimony, character, writings, evidence, relevancy and its limits. Readers who wish further information on federal American rules of evidence may go to www.uscourts.gov and for Canada www.canlii.org.

Government law, unlike religious law, demands immediate accountability. The police are the enforcement arm of government. In the secular law there is a penalty exacted for an infraction of the law. Religion's laws, however, for the most part, are empty pious statements. The only religious law penalties are often denial of the sacraments, excommunication, refusal to marry a divorced person, or perform some other service, or stripping a religious institution from its religious designation, if it performs an act contrary to the religion's doctrine. The threat of not being saved by a religion is just that- a threat- a threat that can only be acted upon in the supernatural world, except for Islamic governments operating under Sharia law, where infractions are meted out in the real world.

Whereas the revelations or rulings of the courts, for infractions of the law, are determined by using the rules of evidence, inspired by men in the real world, and judgment day occurs in the real world, the infractions of the revelations from the Bible on morals and ethics (Ten Commandments, Beatitudes, and Christian virtues)written by men two thousand years ago, inspired by a Holy Spirit, are not determined by clerics in the real world, but only by God on judgment day in the supernatural world.

4. The Pillar of Faith That God (Judge), or the Sons of God (Jurors Will Fortune Tell the Correct Penalties and Rewards Based upon the Court's Rules of Evidence.

Christianity fortune tells that if you do not obey its laws, upon what kind of life you must live in this world, through counsel on good and evil, as found in the Bible, or other sacred books, as derived from God in the supernatural world believers will not gain entry into the supernatural world- the Hereafter, but will face punishment on judgment day in the supernatural world.

The courts, in their fortune telling promise speedy trials, justice for the victim, and punishment for the accused. Heaven, for an accused, who appears before the courts, is being found not guilty of breaking the law, and Hell for the accused if found guilty. Hell for the victim is when the accused is found not guilty of breaking the law and heaven for the victim, if the accused is found guilty. Whereas Heaven and Hell for the courts of the government are known, Heaven and Hell for religion are places of mystery. No one in religion has ever seen Heaven or Hell but there is much discussion among believers about Heaven and Hell.

The courts of government recognize that there are many shades of justice- that the revelations of judges and juries of the secular courts are not absolute and eternal, as they are for religion, by allowing unsuccessful litigants the opportunity to appeal, whereas in Christianity right and wrong is known, as found in the Bible. Judges of the courts are the Gods of the real world. You can be found not guilty, guilty, one-half, one-quarter, or one-tenth guilty, through plea bargaining, unlike in Christianity under God's law, there is no bargaining with God.

Both the government's laws, and the courts rulings are relative, as they reflect the morals of a particular time in our history. Contrary to popular opinion, there is no such thing as absolute truth or justice in the real world, only the appearance of justice for the secular law, as provided by judges and sometimes juries, as there are no universal, uniform laws, or universal penalties, or universal rules of evidence in determining infractions of the law. Laws with their penalties and rewards may vary from culture to culture from country to country, and within countries from state to state, or from province to province. The actual disposition of the law will depend upon individual circumstances, personalities, and the mores of the time.

Justice will only be achieved if there is an equal access to financial resources and competent knowledgeable litigants acting on behalf of the parties, including competent judges and juries of the courts. Justice will be influenced by the social status of both the victims and the accused. If you feel that justice has been exacted, that you have equality before the law, you then believe that justice has been secured, and that you have equality before the law. If you feel that justice has not been served, or you do not have equality before the law, then justice has not been served. It is only the individual's perception in making that determination that is real. There is no external, universal worldly measuring stick, outside of an individual's own perception, that is able to determine if you have received justice, or have equal benefit before the law. Justice, therefore, is an illusion, contrary to the claims of courts, politicians and their demagogic leaders. It is only religions that know what is right and wrong. Religions need no rules of evidence in determining justice. For religion, truth is known, and justice will be absolute and certain.

THE THREE MARKETING PILLARS OF DEMOCRATIC GOVERNMENT COURTS

1. The Pillar of Worship of Idols (Great Judges of the Past)

A necessary condition for accepting the relative revelations of the courts in dispensing justice, will not only be reliance upon faith in the wisdom of the Gods, and sons of God for the Courts, but regular practice in the worshiping of idols- the great thinkers of the courts, whether it be a Supreme court justice, or other great jurist, past or present, not unlike in religion, where there is regular practice in the worshiping of God, Jesus, a Pope, Muhammad, Ayatollah, prophets, or saints of religion, and for government in the worshiping of the founding fathers of government or a President or Prime Minister.

2. The Pillar of Periodic Pilgrimages to One's Holy Places

Like the purveyors of religion, judges make annual pilgrimages to their holy places. For the courts, such pilgrimages take the form of the annual meetings of their respective judicial associations, where much discussion is held on how to improve their positions of power and prestige by enhancing the quality of their revelations, and the size of their pensions. If accused by believers of judicial misconduct, they make periodic pilgrimages to their self regulating Judicial Councils, whose role is supposed to serve the public interest, but often such judicial councils engage in misconduct, as they are unable to separate their self-interest from the self interest of protecting fellow judges.

3. The Pillar of Sorcery (Ritual, Magic and Ceremony) to Convince Believers That Judges Are God, and That Jurors Are the Sons of God.

For revealed religion, sorcery is practiced in regular and special worship services, where the priest, minister, rabbi or imam dress in many colors, and fancy hats, and in some cases wave censors, emitting incense, laying on of hands, and use various other forms of ritual to impress their believers. For revealed religion this may also include chanting, praying, meditation, singing hymns, reciting passages from their sacred books, and the use of special symbols in their séances, such as- a crucifix, Star of David, or crescent moon. This sorcery often convinces believers in some jurisdictions to support the establishment of religious schools to indoctrinate the young, as the future makers of offerings to their religion. (Appendix C)

For the courts, similar elements of witchcraft are displayed, as in religion, and government, in dress of the participants; standing upon entry, and exit of the judge; addressing the judge as your honor; swearing to tell the truth, and the display of government, and court symbols and images. Most of the chanting and yelling is done between the bench and the different litigants. In criminal cases the defendant is often placed in a special seat, or box, or cage, and often accompanied by a person dressed in special garb, carrying a gun, as a symbol of authority. There is great fear and awe- the accused, in fear of the person dressed in special garb, carrying a gun, and the prosecution and defense attorneys, in great awe of the Judge.

PART 1V
RECOMMENDATIONS

SECULAR LAW SUPREME

If the world is to be saved from the different conflicts between the world's different religions and governments, all democratic nation states must ensure, where the laws of the State, and religion are in conflict, that the laws of the State are supreme, and not the dogma of any particular religion, notwithstanding that the legitimacy for the laws of the State was created by government oligarchies, disguised as democracies. Oligarchies have some form of legitimacy, whereas the legitimacy of the Christian religion is based upon reports of some men two thousand years ago, alleged to have been received from God by the angel Gabriel, inspired by a Holy Spirit (dove and tongues of fire). The challenge for western government oligarchies, disguised as democracies, is to respect the right of religions to promote their particular brand of speculation and make believe, morals and ethics, while at the same time requiring religions to respect the secular laws of society.

FREEDOM OF RELIGION

The freedom of religion provision in democratic government constitutions resulted from earlier belief that the claims of religion were true. Modern day science has provided evidence to show that many of those earlier claims of religion are not true. The Roman Catholic Church has acknowledged that in the book of Genesis, the writers of the Bible did not write as scientists, but as writers of religious "truth" in claiming that God created the universe in six days, and rested on the seventh. The Roman Catholic Church has now tacitly acknowledged that the first man and women was not Adam and Eve, that humans evolved through organic processes, as found in the fossil and genetic record. Christian scholars, who do not depend upon the collection plate for sustenance, as does your local priest and minister have because of the literalistic burden of the gospels on the virgin birth and divinity of Jesus, relocated the gospels to their proper function as myths and stories.

As the earlier power of religion has been minimized by this increased scientific and religious knowledge, if the world is to be saved from the atrocities committed by the different religions, it is recommended that the freedom of religion provisions in government constitutions be amended in such a way as to require religion to be subject to the same advertising guidelines, as apply to all other businesses in society in the marketing of their businesses.

Under such circumscription religion would continue to be free to promote its own set of morals and ethics, as any other agency in a free and democratic society -free to influence government on matters, such as- drinking of alcohol, dancing, dating members of other religions, and races; free to speak on sexual conduct, forms of dress in public, the value of life, the sin of homosexuality and euthanasia; marriage between members of the same sex, and different religions, and race; contraception, and the use of drugs in society.

TRANSPARENCY AND ACCOUNTABLILITY

Christian clerics who seek offerings from believers, who ignore the evidence from science, and the evidence from Christian scholars, become subject to the allegation of seeking offerings under false pretences or fraudulently. (Criminal Code of Canada, Part IX-Offences and Rights and Property, s. 365.) Democratic governments that provide tax relief for religious offerings, and that recognize religion in the public sphere as a legitimate authority, would be subject to a finding of being guilty of aiding and abetting that fraudulent behavior. To ensure that Christianity is fully transparent and accountable to believers, it is recommended that democratic governments further amend the Freedom of Religion provision in their constitutions to require Christianity to provide by an independent party one religious service annually the findings of science and Christian scholars. If Christian churches fail to do so democratic governments should end tax relief for believer's offerings.

GOVERNMENT SUBSIDY

Democratic governments currently provide tax relief to believers for their offerings. This, in effect, is a subsidy for the business of religion for its good works in supporting the poor, disadvantaged, ill, and disabled members of society. To ensure that the offerings received by churches are used for such charitable purposes, it is recommended that the government require annually that Churches provide evidence that at least seventy-five percent of such offerings is used for such purposes.

DIRECT DEMOCRACY

With the current technological advances giving rise to the internet, computers, cell phones, and like devices, it is now possible to operate as a true direct democracy, where the public can vote on every issue. Democratic governments would continue to use the crafty science of democracy to elect an oligarchy. The oligarchy would be a forum where the role of the different political parties in the oligarchy would be to provide their positions on any issue, allowing the public to vote using their computer, or cell phone as to which political party position that the public supports.

To facilitate the public in making an informed decision at time of election of a new government, it is recommended that an independent body of parliament be established, whose role it would be to provide to the public the performance of the elected government on its promises, so as the public will be able to properly assess the future credibility of the party if re-elected as the government.

WORLD GOVERNMENT

A fundamental drive of humans is self-interest in securing the energy of life, and life's other amenities. Capitalism, or the free enterprise system, serves that individual self-interest. However, there is a contradiction between the goals of capitalism, serving self-interest, and the goal of western government oligarchies, in disguise as democracies, pretending to represent the people in serving the public good. The challenge for individual democratic governments, pretending to be representing all the people, is to balance the individual private self interest of capitalism with the goal of democratic governments in serving the public good.

If the world is to be saved from all the atrocities committed in the name of western government oligarchies, disguised as democracies, in the competition for the world's economic resources, it is recommended that democratic governments surrender their individual sovereignty economic interests to a world government, equitably allocating the economic resources of the world, operating under the rule of law with a central judiciary, supported by a world police force to enforce the will of the central government in serving the common good of the individual constituent governments.

MEDIA REPORTING

It is the role of the media to hold governments accountable. If the media is to be effective in holding democratic governments accountable in reporting relations of democratic governments with other governments, it is important that both sides of any issue be told. This can only be effectively done, if the media uses in addition to its own government sources, actual sources from those other governments, and not simply dissidents from those other governments.

FINANCIAL RESOURCES

It is recommended that where a private citizen feels that governments at all levels and its agencies has wronged him, and there is probable cause to support such wrong, that a private citizen be provided by the court such financial assistance as may be necessary to provide a level playing field between the parties to ensure that justice is seen to have been done.

CONCLUSION

The legitimacy for democratic governments, pretending to represent the people, is that they use the crafty science of democracy to determine who are members of the oligarchy, whereas for Christianity, pretending to represent God, there is little or no democratic legitimacy, as believers have little, or no say in determining who are the supreme leaders of the theocracy. Although western government oligarchies, in disguise as democracies, and their courts, use many of the same pillars and elements of the legal definition of witchcraft-crafty science, sorcery, and fortune telling, and rely upon faith in seeking payment of taxes from believers, as does Christianity in seeking offerings from believers, the foundations for their respective pillars are vastly different.

Whereas the existence of God, the foundation of Christianity, is unknown, and the Christian God is unaccountable, the secular God and sons of God for democratic governments, and their courts are known and accountable. Whereas for Christianity, the revelation of the Bible is alleged to have been communicated to men inspired by a Holy Spirit from God, for western government oligarchies, in disguise as democracies, the revelations of their Bibles (constitutions) were created by the rules of legislative procedure, and needed no inspiration from a Holy Spirit for their creation. Whereas for religion justice for violation of its morals and ethics is claimed to be meted out on judgment day in a Hereafter in a supernatural world, for the courts of western governments, the revelations (rulings) of judges and juries are created by using the court's rules of evidence, and although justice may be an illusion, judgment day occurs in the real world.

It is the use of witchcraft by Christianity that convinces believers in the existence of God and the son of God in the supernatural world, as it is for democratic governments and their courts in convincing believers that they are God and the sons of God in the real world. Without faith in the existence and power of God, and the son(s) of God, although the concept of faith is without foundation, and the opposite of reason, believers would not accept the legitimacy and power of religions, democratic governments, and their courts without faith. The world would be doomed to anarchy. Faith is the cement necessary for believers to accept the authority and governance of religions, western government oligarchies, in disguise as democracies, and justice in their courts. This is the central message that the reader can gain from "Everyman's Prayer Book: Democratic Governments and their Courts- the Other Great Religions."

APPENDIX A -
THE CHRISTIAN VIRTUES

Cleanliness:2 Corinthians 7:1 - Since we have these promises, beloved, let us cleanse ourselves from every defilement of body and spirit, and make holiness perfect in fear of the Lord.

Cheerfulness: Philippians 4: 4- Rejoice in the Lord always; again I will say, Rejoice.

Cheerfulness: Colossians 3: 16-Let the word of Christ dwell in you richly, teach and admonish one another in all wisdom, and sing psalms and hymns and spiritual songs with thankfulness in your hearts to God,17, And whatever you do, in word or deed, do everything in the name of the Lord Jesus, giving thanks to God and the Father through him.

Courage: Philippians 1: 27- Only let your manner of life be worthy of the gospel of Christ, so that whether I come and see you or am absent, I may hear of you that you stand firm in one spirit, with one mind striving side by side for the faith of the gospel, 28, and not frightened in anything by your opponents. This is a clear omen to them of their destruction, but of your salvation, and that from God.

Diligence: Romans 12:11, Never flag in zeal, be aglow with the spirit, serve the Lord.

Discretion: Ephesians 5: 15, Look carefully then how you walk, not as unwise men but as wise, 16 making the most of the time, because the days are evil,17, Therefore do not be foolish, but understand what the will of the Lord is.

Endurance:2 Timothy 2, First of all, then, I urge that supplications, prayer, intercessions, and thanksgivings be made for all men 2, for kings and all who are in high positions, that we may lead a quiet and peaceable life, godly and respectful in every way, 3, This is good, and it is acceptable in the sight of God our saviour

Faith: Mark 11: 22, and the seven left no children. Last of all the women also died. 23, In the resurrection whose wife will she be? For the seven had her as wife. 24, Jesus said to them "Is this not why you are wrong, that you know neither the scriptures nor the power of God."

Faithfulness: 1 Corinthians 4:2, Moreover it is required of stewards that they be found trustworthy

Forgiveness: Ephesians 4: 31, Let all bitterness and wrath, and anger and clamour and slander be put away from you, with all malice, 32, and be kind to one another, tender-hearted, forgiving one another, as God in Christ forgave you.

Friendliness: Romans 12: 15, Rejoice with those who rejoice, weep with those who weep, 16, Live in harmony with one another; do not be haughty, but associate with the lowly; never be conceited,17, Repay no one evil for evil, but take thought for what is noble in the sight of all,18, If possible, so far as it depends upon you, live peacefully with all.

Gratitude: Philippians 4: 6, Have no anxiety about anything, but in everything by prayer and supplication with thanksgiving let your requests be known to God

Honesty: Romans 12:17, Repay no one evil for evil, but take thought for what is noble in the sight of all

Honour: Peter 2:17, Honour all men. Love the brotherhood. Fear God. Honour the emperor.

Humility: Philippians 2: 3, Do nothing from selfishness or deceit, but in humility count others better than yourselves. 4, Let each of you look not only to his own self- interest, but also to the interest of others. 5, Have this mind among yourselves, which is yours in Jesus Christ, 6, who, though he was in the form of God, did not count equality with God a thing to be grasped, 7, but emptied himself, taking the form of a servant, being born in the likeness of men, 8, And being found in human form he humbled himself and became obedient until death, even death on a cross. 9,Therefore God has highly exalted him and bestowed upon him the name which is above every name, 10, that at the name of Jesus every name should bow, in heaven and on earth and under the earth, 11, and every tongue confess that Jesus Christ is Lord, to the glory of God the Father.

Liberality: 2 Corinthians 9: 6, by purity, knowledge, forbearance, kindness, the Holy Spirit, genuine love, 7 truthful speech and the power of God; with the weapons of righteousness for the right hand and for the left; 8 in honour and dishonour, in ill repute and good repute. We are treated as impostors, and yet are true; 9 as unknown, and yet well known; as dying, and behold we live; as punished, and yet not killed; 10 as sorrowful, yet always rejoicing; as poor, yet making many rich; as having nothing, and yet possessing everything. 11, Our mouth is open to you, Corinthians ; our heart is wide. 12, You are not restricted by us, but you are restricted in in your own affections. 13, In return - I speak as to children - widen your hearts also. 14, Do not be mismated with unbelievers. For what partnership have righteousness and iniquity? Or what fellowship has light with darkness? 15, What accord has Christ with Belial? Or what has a believer have in common with a unbeliever?

Love:1 John 4: 7- He came for testimony, to bear witness to the light, 8, He was not the light, but came to bear witness to the light.

Meekness: Matthew 5:5, Blessed are the meek for they shall inherit the earth

Obedience: Romans 13:1, Let every person be subject to the governing authorities. For there is no authority except from God, and those that exist have been instituted by God 2, Therefore he who resists the authorities resists what God has appointed, and those wh resist will incur judgement, 3, For rulers are not a terror to good conduct, but to bad. Would you have no fear of him who is in authority? Then do what is good and you will receive his approval, 4,for he is God's servant for your good. But if you do wrong, be afraid, for he does not bear the sword in vain; he is the servant of God to execute his wrath on the wrongdoer,5, Therefore one must be subject, not only to avoid God's wrath, but also for the sake of conscience. 6, For the same reason you also pay taxes, for the authorities are the ministers of God; attending to this very thing. 7, Pay all of them their dues, taxes to whom taxes are due, revenue to whom revenue is due, respect to whom respect is due, honour to whom honour is due.

Patience: Hebrews 10: 36, For you have need of endurance, so that you may do the will of God and receive what is promised. 37, "For yey a little while, and the coming one shall come shall not tarry;

Peacefulness: Romans 12: 18, If possible, so far as it depends upon you, live peacefully with all.

Prudence: James 1:19, Know this, my beloved brethren. Let every man be quick to hear, slow to speak, slow to anger

Pure thinking: Philippians 4: 8, Finally, brethren, whatever is true, whatever is honourable, whatever is just, whatever is pure, whatever is lovely, whatever is gracious, if there is any excellence, if there is anything worthy of praise, think about these things

Purity: 2 Timothy 2:22, So shun youthful passions and aim at righteousness, faith, love, and peace, along with those who call upon the Lord from a pure heart.

Steadfastness: Ephesians 6: 10, Finally be strong in the Lord and in the strength of the might. 11, Put on the whole armour of God, that you may be able to stand against the wiles of the devil. 12, For we are not contending against flesh and blood, but against the principalities, against the powers, against the world rulers of this present darkness against the spiritual hosts of wickedness in the heavenly places. 13,

Therefore take the whole armour of God, that you may be able to withstand in the evil day, and having done all, to stand. 14, Stand therefore, having girded your loins with truth, and having put on the breastplate of righteousness. 15, and having shod your feat with the equipment of the gospel of peace; 16, besides all theses, taking the shield of faith, with which you can quench all the flaming darts of evil one. 17, And take the helmet of salvation, and the sword of spirit, which is the word of God. 18, Pray at all times in the spirit, with all prayer and supplication. To that end keep alert with all perseverance, making supplication for all the saints

Sympathy: 1 Peter 3: 8, Finally, all of you, have unity of spirit, sympathy, love of the brethren, a tender heart and a humble mind. 9, Do not return evil for evil or reviling for reviling; but on the contrary bless, for to this you have been called, that you may obtain a blessing.

Temperance: 1 Corinthians 9: 25, Every athlete exercises self control in all things. They do it to receive a perishable wreath, but we are imperishable.26, Well, I do not run aimlessly, I do not box as one beating the air; 27, but I pommel my body and subdue it, lest after preaching to others I myself should be disqualified.

Truthfulness: Ephesians 4: 15, Rather, speaking the truth in love, we are to grow up in every way into him who is the head, into Christ, 25, Therefore, putting away falsehood, let everyone speak the truth with his neighbour, for we are members of another, 29, Let no evil talk come out of your mouths, but only such as is good for edifying, as fits the occasion, that it may impart grace to those who hear.

Source: New Testament, Psalms and Proverbs, page xxv, The Gideons International in Canada, 501 Imperial Road, Guelph, Ontario, Canada, as quoted from The Holy Bible, Revised Standard Version, 1971, Canadian Bible Society, 1835 Yonge St., Toronto 7, Ontario, Canada.

APPENDIX B -
AN ODE TO OUR SUN

Oh Holy Sun,
Beware of false witness to other Gods,
For you are the Almighty creator of Earth
And all living things.

Blessed art thou among stars.
Blessed is the fruit of thy inner core-
Carbon, hydrogen, nitrogen and oxygen.

We thank thee for the radiation you emit from your photosphere,
For it is this sunlight,
And the heavy atomic elements,
That you and other stars have created at high temperatures,
That provides for us, our universe's architecture,
And gives us our life.

Oh holy Sun, we know that your life is not eternal,
That you will die,
That you will shed your particles of matter out into space,
And these particles will be born again,
As your children in other stars

But as humans we will not die,
For we will journey to planets of other solar systems,
And when all stars die,
And all planets become uninhabitable to life,
We will become God,
And we will live forever!

APPENDIX C -
RELIGIOUS DISCRIMINATION

The legislators in writing the American Constitution in 1767, in order to resolve the conflict between the different Christian religions in governing the nation, provided a clear separation of Church and State. In Canada, one hundred years later in 1867, the legislators took a different approach in resolving the conflict between the different Christian religions, by embedding in the Canadian Constitution, Section 93, the funding of the Protestant and Roman Catholic religious schools, which were in operation at the time of union of upper and lower Canada.

It was only the Roman Catholic religion, as a result of numbers, and its monolithic authoritarian structure, that would be able to establish a full fledged separate school system. Protestant religions, on the other hand, because of their fragmentation, and obedience to no recognized central authority, were unable to sustain any like establishment of separate schools, and over time for the most part accepted the separation of Church and State. As a result the current religious discrimination occurred not through the fault of the Catholic Church, but through the inability of Protestant sects to establish their own religious schools.

With the later funding of French language school boards in Ontario the enrolment base for Ontario's schools became in many areas of the province divided among four public school boards. In 2007 the Ontario Progressive Conservative party promised that if elected it would publicly fund other religious schools and further divide the enrolment base of Ontario's into more than four school boards. As the Conservative party was not elected this thankfully did not happen, as the cost of education, and the quality of education for Ontario students would have been further compromised.

As after one hundred and forty seven years, Canada and Ontario have become a much more multi-religious, and multi-cultural society, the continued public funding of Roman Catholic schools has become a costly anomaly affecting the quality of education of students in the operation of four school boards, particularly in non urban low population or low density areas of the province, affecting grade organization in elementary schools, available program options in secondary schools, and provision of special facilities and programs in both elementary and secondary schools. To reduce the costs and improve the quality of education for students, ending the public funding of the Roman Catholic school system condemned by the United Nations Human Rights Tribunal, as religious discrimination, becomes necessary.

To address the issue, as the Ontario Liberal party was to table its 2014 budget, I sought from the leaders, and all the members of the Ontario legislative assembly to address the estimated two billion dollar cost in the public funding of four school systems, as the division of enrolment between four boards reduces the quality of education of students in the four school systems, and I received no response. At the same time, I appealed to the Ontario Assembly of Catholic Bishops, as moral leaders to observe the Golden Rule, "Do unto others as you would have them do unto you", and to obey Jesus' second greatest Commandment "Love thy neighbor as thy self" by initiating action with Ontario's political parties to effect change, but they failed to respond.

The continued public funding of the Roman Catholic religion has become even more troubling, as Christian scholars, who have no financial interest, as does your local priest or minister in seeking offerings from believers, in their book titled "The Acts of Jesus", because of literalistic burden of the gospels, relocated them to their proper function as myths and stories. In effect, the only continuing purpose in the public funding of the Roman Catholic religion in Ontario's schools is the promotion of the catechism and the myths and stories to ensure the collection of offerings from each new generation of believers to support the business of the Roman Catholic religion.

APPENDIX D - EVOLUTION OF THE UNIVERSE

Scientists have determined that the universe began with a Big Bang 18 plus billion years ago, where space, the basic particles, and forces of the universe were created- over time forming all the stars and galaxies in the universe, including our planet earth, and life itself. Science has found no evidence that the Big Bang was caused by a supernatural God. Science has only been able to explain how the universe has evolved based upon what it has been able to observe from telescopes, and confirm in its science laboratories.

Scientists have determined that the universe today consists of approximately 73 % hydrogen and 25 % helium atoms, with the remaining 2 % heavier elements (atoms), of which carbon is one, being created by nuclear fusion of massive stars. Scientists have determined that when massive stars collapse through gravity in a supernova, the heavier elements, along with the lighter elements, become part of a spinning gas cloud, and when overcome again by gravity the spinning gas cloud forms a secondary star, of which our Sun is believed to be one.

Scientists believe that in the forming of our Sun, that the light elements of hydrogen and helium formed the gaseous planets, such as- Jupiter and Neptune and the heavier elements, such as- iron, nickel, carbon, and so on,formed Mars, Venus and our planet Earth, from which life began based upon the carbon atom. Scientists have estimated that our Sun will burn all of its hydrogen in about four (4) billion years from now, and die, but humans will die many years before, as our Sun will balloon in size before it dies, killing all life on Earth in a heat death, before the Sun actually dies. Scientists have determined that the same fate will occur to all the other stars in the universe when they burn all of their hydrogen, or alternatively the universe will collapses upon itself beforehand, if the dark energy, or anti-gravity of space expansion (71%) does not achieve a balance between the opposite force of gravity of the known visible (5%) and dark matter(24%) in space.

Scientists have determined that life arose based primarily upon the carbon atom, as the carbon atom can easily join with other atoms to form complex life, and that our bodies contain much of the same matter, as contained in the stars, galaxies, and the gas clouds of the universe. As our planet Earth includes the temperature, oxygen and water necessary for the origin of life, single cell life began about 3.7 billion years ago, shortly after the creation of our planet Earth, and complex multi-cellular life only arose about 400 million years ago.

From that multi-cellular life early man developed about six million years ago, and modern man, Homo sapiens, only came upon the scene about 200,000 years ago, through the process of natural selection as outlined by Charles Darwin, which is supported by the fossil, and genetic record. Scientists have determined that the plant and animal food that we eat consists mainly of the same atoms- hydrogen, oxygen, carbon, nitrogen, calcium, and iron, as found in the dust particles, stars, and galaxies of the universe. Scientists have determined that the plant food that we eat, resulted from photosynthesis, through the light wavelength of the electromagnetic radiation from our Sun, of which the other five wavelengths are- radio, infrared, ultraviolet, x-ray, and gamma ray.

Scientists have determined that the same electromagnetic force, consisting of negatively charged electrons and positively charged protons, is responsible for the beating of our heart, and our ability to see is based upon the visible light wavelength of that same electromagnetic force interacting with the chemical elements in our eyes. Scientists have determined that humans are interconnected to all the forces in the universe- the strong and weak nuclear forces operating at the subatomic level, the electromagnetic force providing the heat, and light energy for life at both the macro and micro levels, and the gravitational force holding all the matter together in the universe from flying off into space.

Scientists have recently found over one hundred Earth like planets outside our local galaxy the Milky Way, some of which may have the necessary characteristics for life- temperature, water and oxygen and a magnetic field protecting the planet from the radiation of its Sun. The magnetic field for our Earth (7,918 mi. diameter) based upon seismographic evidence is believed to result from Earth's hard solid iron outer core, inner core of liquid iron and nickel (1400 mile deep, 8000 F), hard rocky mantle(lower mantle 4000 F), and crust. As our Earth rotates counter clockwise, it is believed that the conductive heat from the hard iron outer core, and the convection heat from the boiling liquid inner core, and Earth's lower mantle, that creates the dynamo effect. It is this dynamo effect that produces Earth's magnetic field of positively charged protons and negatively charged electrons, that protects us from the gamma and x-ray radiation from our Sun allowing life to occur. (Discover, July-August 2014, pages 35-41) If life is possible on other planets, it would also need not only the necessary temperature, water and oxygen, but also a magnetic field to protect life from its Sun.

BIBLIOGRAPHY

GENERAL

Government of Canada, Consumer and Corporate Affairs: Competition Act, Special Edition 1991.

Government of Canada, Misleading Representations and Deceptive Marketing Practices: What are the Possible Penalties? Cat. No. RG52-29/10-2000, reprinted February 2002

Government of the United States, Federal Trade Act, Washington, D.C., FTC Policy Statement on Deception, October 14, 1983.

Bryson, Bill, A Short History of Nearly Everything, Broadway Books, New York, 2003, a Division of Random House

Cook, Michael, A Brief History of the Human Race, W.W. Norton & Company, Inc., 500 Fifth Ave., New York, N.Y. 10110

RELIGION

Bunson, Matthew, General Editor, 2010 Catholic Almanac, Our Sunday Visitor Inc., Huntington, Indiana 46750

Cantor, Norman F., Civilization of the Middle Ages, Harper Collins Publishers, Inc., East 53rd Street, New York, NY, 10022

Elton, G. R., Reformation Europe, 1517-1559, Harper & Row, Publishers, New York

Flower, Liz, The Elements of World Religions, Elements Books Inc., PO Box 830,Rockport, MA, 01966

Frost, Jr., S.E., Basic Teachings of the Great Philosophers, Bantam Doubleday Dell Publishing Group, Inc., 1540 Broadway, New York, NY, 10036

Funk, Robert W. The Acts of Jesus, A Polebridge Press Book, Harper Collins

Heeren, Fred, Show Me God, Searchlight Publications, Wheeling, Illinois

Kung, Hans, and others, Christianity and the World Religions, Doubleday, 1540 Broadway, New York, NY, 10036

Martin, Michael, The Case Against Christianity, Temple University Press, Philadelphia 19122

McKenzie, John L., SJ, The Roman Catholic Church, Holt Rinehart & Winston, NY., 1969 p.124-124 and 126

Packard, Jerrold M., Peter's Kingdom, Charles Scribner's Sons, New York

Popkin and Stroll, Philosophy Made Simple, Bantam Doubleday Dell Publishing Group, Inc., 1540 Broadway, New York, NY, 10036

The Holy Bible, Revised Standard Version, 1971, Canadian Bible Society, 1835 Yonge St., Toronto 7, Ontario, Canada

Warburton, Nigel, Philosophy: The Basics, Routledge, 29 West 35th Street, New York, NY,10001

Armstrong, Karen, A History of God, Alfred A. Knopf Inc., New York

Barbour, Ian G., When Science Meets Religion, HarperSanFrancisco, Harper Collins Publishers, Inc., East 53rd Street, New York, NY, 10022

SCIENCE

Bodanis, David, E=mc², Berkley Publishing Group, 375 Hudson Street, New York, New York, 10014

Chaisson, Eric and Steve McMillan, Astronomy Today, Prentice Hall Inc, Upper Saddle River, NJ 07458

Darwin, Charles, The Origin of Species by means of Natural Selection, and The Descent of Man and Selection in relation to Sex, Encyclopaedis Britannica, Inc., Toronto, Chicago and London

Davies, Paul, The Mind of God, Touchtone, Rockefeller Centre, 1230 Avenue of the Americas, New York, NY, 10020

Davis, Paul, God and the New Physics, Simon and Schuster Inc. Rockefeller Centre, 1230 Avenue of the Americas, New York, New York, 10020

Dawkins, Richard, The Blind Watchmaker, W.W. Norton and Company, Inc., 500 Fifth Avenue, New York, N.Y. 10110

Delsemme, Armand, Our Cosmic Origins, From the Big Bang to the emergence of life and intelligence, Cambridge University Press, 1998, 40 West 20th Street, New York, N.Y. 10011-4211

Ferris, Timothy, The Whole Shebang, Simon & Schuster, Rockefeller Centre, 1230 Avenue of the Americas, New York, NY, 10020

Goldsmith, Donald, Einstein's Greatest Blunder?, Harvard University Press, Cambridge, Massachusetts

Hawking, Stephen, A Brief History of Time, Bantam Doubleday Dell Publishing Group, Inc., 1540 Broadway, New York, NY, 10036

Jenkins, Morton, Evolution, NTC/Contemporary Publishing, 4255 West Touhy Avenue, Lincolnwood (Chicago), Illinois, 60646-1975, USA

Jones, Steve, The Language of Genes, Anchor Books, Doubleday, 1540 Broadway, New York, NY, 10036

Krauss, Laurence M., Atom: An Odyssey from the Big Bang to Life on Earth and Beyond, Little Brown & Company, New York, NY

Leakey, Richard, The Origin of Humankind, Basicbooks, 10 East 53rd St., New York, NY, 10022-5299

Rees, Martin, Just Six Numbers, Basicbooks, 10 East 53rd St., New York, NY, 10022-5299

Ridley, Matt, Genome, Harper Collins, Harper Collins Publishers, Inc., East 53rd Street, New York, NY, 10022

Sykes, Bryan, The Seven Daughters of Eve, W.W. Norton and Company, Inc., 500 Fifth Avenue, New York, N.Y. 10110, 2002

Thompson, Mel, Eastern Philosophy, NTC/Contemporary Publishing, 4255 West Touhy Avenue, Lincolnwood (Chicago), Illinois, 60646-1975, USA

Adams, Fred, Origins of Existence, The Free Press, A Division of Simon & Schuster, Inc., 1230 Avenue of the Americas, New York, N.Y. 10020

Bruce Thompson, Book Editor, Evolution, Fact or Fiction, Greenhaven Press, 27500 Drake Rd., Farmington Hills, MI, 48331-3535

Robert T. Pennock, Tower of Babel, The Evidence against the New Creationism, The MIT Press, Cambridge, Massachusetts

Silk, Joseph, A Short History of the Universe, W. H. Freeman and company, 41 Madison Avenue, New York, NY, 10010

Discover, 21027 Crossroads Circle, P.O. Box 1612 Waukesha, WI 53187-1612